He Said It!
I Did It!

Lessons from My Father on Mastering Personal Finance

by

Charles W. Buffington III
and
Charles W. Buffington, Jr.

He Said It! I Did It!

Lessons from My Father on Mastering Personal Finance

by
Charles W. Buffington III
and
Charles W. Buffington, Jr.

Copyright © 2005
Charles W. Buffington III and Charles W. Buffington, Jr.
All rights reserved.

ISBN: 1-891773-63-1

Printed in the United States of America

10 9 8 7 6 5 4 3 2 1

Publishing Services Provided By
Orman Press, Inc.
Lithonia, Georgia

Dedication

This book is dedicated to the Proverbs 31 women in our life, whose stewardship laid the financial and spiritual foundation for the life and learning that we share in this book.

Mrs. Minnie Buffington, wife to Charles, Jr. and mother of Charles III, whose sacrifice and hard work has built and managed our family and home for thirty-five years.

Mrs. Fannie Mae Buffington, mother of Charles, Jr. and paternal grandmother of Charles III, whose generosity and love taught us the importance of family.

Mrs. Cora Grimsley, mother-in-law of Charles, Jr. and maternal grandmother to Charles III, who gave us a living example of stewardship in raising nine children on the single income of her husband, independent of charity or governmental assistance.

Mrs. Minnie Bennett Buffington, paternal grandmother of Charles, Jr. and paternal great grandmother of Charles III, who showed us the benefits of managing finances using godly principles.

Mrs. Susan Buffington, wife to Charles III, who is a conscientious, frugal wife, and a tremendous partner on our journey to abundance.

Each of these great women leaves a legacy of stewardship worthy of emulation. We honor them and pray God's richest blessing upon their work.

Acknowledgements

I have received great encouragement for this work from many friends and supporters. I am particularly grateful for the contribution of my two "Pauls"—Dr. Crawford Loritts and my pastor, Dr. George O. McCalep, Jr. I am grateful to my good friend and brother, Dr. Crawford Loritts, for the time he spent reviewing this work and providing advice. I thank Pastor McCalep for his faith in selecting me to serve as chairman of our church's Stewardship Ministry, and for helping us get this work into print through his company, Orman Press.

Finally, to my son, Charles W. Buffington, III, whose faith and persistence gave birth to this work, thank you. Your willingness to be transparent and open to help others realize God's purpose is commendable.

Yours in Christ,
Charles W. Buffington, Jr.

Acknowledgements

In keeping with the title and theme of the book, I would like to thank both my earthly father and my Heavenly Father. My earthly father has been an inspiration to me. He has been a great source of wisdom as the foundation for the book and a strong, steady influence throughout the creative process. I would like to thank my Heavenly Father for making all things possible.

Next, I must acknowledge the two most important women in my life—my wife, Susan, and my mom, Minnie. Susan supported my efforts from the very beginning. Her faith in me and her encouragement kept me going when I was tired and unsure. In spite of her tremendous workload, she proofed the manuscript and offered excellent input. My mom was always there to support and encourage me, also. She proofread my many revisions and provided invaluable insight and perspective. To my team, my family, I love you dearly.

I would also like to thank others who helped give birth to this book—Lynn Holmes-Ross, Doug Keipper, Andi Cutshaw, and Cheryl Edwards, our editor. Thank you to the many friends and family who have provided moral support throughout this process.

Warmest regards,
Charles W. Buffington III

Table of Contents

Foreword

It has been my joy to know Charles Buffington, Jr. for more than twenty years. He is one of my dearest friends. Through the years we have spent many hours together in prayer, planning meetings, ministering together and just "hanging out" with each other. You're not in his presence long before you are struck with his love for and commitment to Jesus Christ, and his desire to apply biblical principles to every area of his life. He loves to share with others what God has taught him.

Along his journey, God has honored Charles and his family because he has, in very practical ways, placed Jesus Christ in first place in his life. He would be the first to humbly tell you that he has been blessed beyond measure. Charles is a very successful businessman who realizes that his accomplishments come as a result of his relationship with Christ and the application of God's Word to life's challenges and opportunities. This is what he calls *stewardship*, and rightly so.

Charles has nurtured and discipled his son, Charles III, with these principles of biblical stewardship. Charles III has picked up the torch and is running with it. Like his dad, he has a desire to share what he has learned with others. In fact, in recent years, they have been teaching these principles to groups and churches across the country. The response is not only gratifying, but lives and families have been literally changed! They both felt the need to share these practical, life-changing principles with a broader audience. And this book, *He Said It! I Did It!*, is the result.

I love the way this book is written! The principles and concepts are not dished out in a theoretical way, but they are wrapped in human experience. I love the refreshing honesty with which this father and son write. Charles III does not shy away from sharing some of his failures, and in so doing, he gives all of us hope. If we will humble ourselves and submit to the power of the Holy Spirit and the authority of God's Word literally, what the Buffingtons share in this book will change our lives.

You are holding in your hands one of those rare resources that you will find yourself referring to time and again, and sharing with others. Thank you, Charles and Charles, for this incredible gift!

Dr. Crawford W. Loritts, Jr.
Author, Speaker, Radio Host

Prologue

Before you begin reading this book, let me offer a working definition of financial freedom. Financial freedom is having sufficient material resources to support your lifestyle and worthwhile causes, independent of employers. In other words, financial freedom means you are not depending on a job to provide your living. You have accumulated wealth that is sufficient to provide for you and your loved ones. When you reach financial freedom, you are working for life and not for a living. You are fulfilling your God-given purpose and enjoying every minute of it. You are working in your area of passion, pursuing higher goals.

The concept of financial freedom took on new meaning for me in the summer of 1995, when I learned the painful lesson that a "good job" is not the same as financial freedom. After twenty-five years of successfully working for one of the largest corporations in the world, I found myself without a job. Like many others, I was downsized, given a little severance package and told farewell. At that point, my wife, Minnie, and I had a choice. We could be victors or victims. We could pursue new horizons or we could spend our energy feeling sorry for ourselves and blaming "them" for "what they did to us." Minnie and I chose to be victors. We set a goal to achieve financial freedom.

This new vision for financial freedom led us to start a business rather than seek employment. We assessed our talents and developed a crude business plan to sell our knowledge and experience. We started a consulting firm, teaching financial principles to churches and helping business organizations improve their marketing and sales. Today, we continue to prosper doing what we love to do, adding value and helping others.

My hope is that you will read this book with the intent of changing your life. Minnie and I are ordinary, everyday people who were set free by following the principles in this book. If we can do it, then you can too.

Charles W. Buffington, Jr.

Introduction

"If a person gets his/her attitude toward money straight, it will
help straighten out almost every other area of his life."

Billy Graham

Prison Cell

In the movie *Shawshank Redemption,* Tim Robbins' character,
Andy Dufresne, is imprisoned for a crime he did not commit, but
he devises a plan to escape. Andy acquires a miniature tool to carve
marble into chess pieces. By day, he carves chess pieces. By night, he
uses the tiny tool to chip away at his cell wall. Andy Dufresne
demonstrates faith and patience, chipping away at the wall every
night for years and years after everyone else has gone to bed.
Twenty years later, he finally tunnels his way to freedom and flees
to a beautiful beach town in Mexico.

Now, imagine yourself in a small, damp prison cell. You can
walk four steps in either direction. Imagine if this is your life! You
look through the bars and see others in a similar prison cell. But
there are some who are roaming free doing interesting, creative, and
challenging things with their lives. Some people are free and others
inhabit small prison cells. They are in bondage and are doing
nothing to escape.

Unfortunately, most Americans are in bondage. If you are
reading this book, you are probably in bondage too. The *American
Heritage Dictionary* defines *bondage* as "a state of being a slave or

servant." Do you have no other choice but to work a job that you hate? Are you bound to your job because you feel you have limited choices? If the answer is yes, you are in bondage.

Imagine if you could pay to get out of bondage. The truth is you can! If you follow the instructions in this book, you can free yourself from the bonds of servitude. Let's think of it this way. Say you need $50,000 and no consumer debt in order to be free to start your own business or do a job that you want to do; not one that you hate and have to do. Think of the job that you have as your slave master. If you could somehow save that $50,000 to pay your debt and the slave master set you free, would you be more motivated to get free? The truth is that you can free yourself. With a little discipline and hard work, you can be free from financial bondage.

Let's shift gears and paint a more positive picture. What would it feel like to go to work every day because you want to and not because you need to? How would your work and financial decisions change if you knew that you did not need your job? How would it feel to sit down to pay your monthly bills and write checks cheerfully, knowing that there is more money where that came from? Now, think about your motivation for working. Is it money? In most cases, it is absolutely about money.

I don't know how many times I hear people say that if they won the lottery they would quit their jobs and do something else. The reason winning the lottery is a prerequisite for quitting their jobs and doing something else is that they do not have a strategy for guiding their financial futures. Many people have more faith in a several-million-to-one chance of winning the lottery than in their own ability to provide the type of lifestyle they desire. We are in bondage, and like in the game of Monopoly, we are wishing for that "get out of jail free" card.

The irony is that we have everything we need to get out of bondage. The key is right in front of us. We just need to use it. We don't have to have six-figure salaries. Our salaries are irrelevant.

All we need is God's Word and the discipline to obey the lessons. Most of the lessons that can free us from financial bondage are common sense, but we struggle to find a way to apply them. We all need help in finding ways to apply wisdom. I have been fortunate enough to have an earthly father who helped me understand the lessons from my Heavenly Father. These lessons helped me become financially free, and now I am sharing them with you. I hope you will apply them so you, too, can be free.

Lessons From My Father

I have read several books about how to get rich, but there was something missing. I started thinking about all of those rich people (celebrities and professional athletes) who were in more bondage than I was. Money alone did not free these people. They had money, but they did not experience abundance. What is the point of being rich when you are still in bondage?

Many of you reading this may be thinking, "How can a rich person be in bondage?" Many of them, even with their large salaries, paint themselves into a corner by consuming so much that they have to continue doing work that may actually be unfulfilling. Some rich people spend their money as if it will continue to flow forever. When they cannot continue to produce at that level, they find themselves in financial hardship. Many are not generous with their blessings and do not find fulfillment in their many toys. They ultimately find themselves on the same treadmill that many of you are on. The reality is some rich people just have bigger prison cells.

I decided that what was missing in the "get rich" books was godly wisdom. The purpose of this book is to show you where the key to your prison cell is and to teach you how to free yourself from bondage. I do not guarantee that you will get rich from applying the lessons in this book. You will most certainly become financially secure by applying these lessons. I do guarantee that applying the lessons in this book will bring you a life of abundance.

In 1998, I found myself in financial bondage. I was between jobs. My credit card debt was huge due to years of spending beyond my means. I lived in a condo that I had just purchased a few months earlier, and I was fearful of not being able to make the payments. To make matters worse, I had no savings. In order to make ends meet until I found another job, I was taking credit card advances to pay my bills. For the first time in my adult life, I was afraid. My choices were to accept any job that was offered to me or risk putting myself in an incredible hole by holding out for a better job.

I was in bondage. I put myself in that position because I had not used my money and resources wisely. My choices were limited. I might have had to take a job I would have been miserable doing just so I could pay my bills. I had painted myself into a corner because of a consistent pattern of poor decisions.

I was scared, but I knew I had to do something. I needed to be resourceful, so I gathered all of my bills and did the math. I determined what I would have to make in my next job in order to maintain a comfortable lifestyle. I started to figure out where I had wasted money, and how much I would need to save so I wouldn't be in this position again. Most of all, I needed counseling, so I went to the most valuable resource available to me—my father.

My father is financially independent. He did not win the lottery. He never signed an NBA or NFL contract, and he never inherited a penny. My father grew up poor in Miami, Florida. He never graduated from college, but he is an extremely intelligent and wise man.

He is a devout Christian who made his share of mistakes along the way. He learned from his mistakes, and he became obedient to God in his personal and financial life. He worked hard and had the discipline to apply the lessons that he learned in order to prosper. At fifty years of age, his homes and cars were paid off. For many years, he was a sales executive, but today, he takes on consulting jobs and business proposals that interest him. He and my mother travel to Europe and Africa on vacation regularly. He plays golf when he wants. He teaches Sunday school and participates in church projects that most people could not do because of work obligations. My father is free.

One afternoon, I stopped by my parents' house to ask his advice. He said, "Son, this personal finance stuff is not rocket science."

"What do you mean? I have been working hard, and I am still in this position. How can I be free of all of this stress and worry?"

My father looked me in the eyes and told me something I will never forget. "You have to remember one thing from this conversation. Be obedient to God's Word, and you will be free." His words really struck me. Could it be that easy?

"It is that easy," he said. "It took me years to figure it out, but once I learned it, everything fell into place." I looked at him with some doubt, but I had to give it some credence since he had accomplished so much.

> "Be obedient to God's Word, and you will be free."

"You can be rich, but God wants us to be abundant," he said with intensity. "You can be rich, but still live in bondage. Charles, you need to understand that God has loaned us everything. We can either make the most of what He has blessed us with or we can squander it. If we are obedient with what He gives us, He gives us more. If I loaned you $10,000 and you turned it into $20,000, I would entrust you with more. God is no different with us."

That only begged the question, "How do you turn $10,000 into $20,000?"

My father replied, "That is the essence of stewardship. You use your time, talent, and treasure to multiply our resources. Each of us has special gifts. We must use those gifts to the best of our ability. We also have a responsibility to make the most of our finances."

He went on to say, "The lessons I am about to teach you are not new. You already intuitively know most of these things. You just need a little guidance. Once I teach you these lessons, apply them, and you will see how God will bless you."

"So you are telling me that if I learn these lessons, and apply them I will be free from all this stress and worry."

"Son, you will be blessed beyond your wildest dreams. Do you think that your mom and I ever thought we would be where we are now twenty years ago? Obedience got us here, and it will get you where you want to be and beyond."

That was a strong endorsement. My father, always the salesman, sold me on the concept. I was anxious to hear what he had to tell me!

"Son, I have ten lessons for you that will change your financial life," my father said, smiling.

Getting in the Game

It was hard for me to believe that I had to hit rock bottom before I tapped into this valuable resource. I was hungry to absorb as much wisdom and knowledge as I could. Hopefully, you are ready to do the same. These lessons from my father will lead you to abundance. I am a living testimony to the power of the lessons in this book. They work. Today, my wife and I have enough saved in our retirement that if we stopped funding it today, at its current growth rate, we would be able to live off of it comfortably in retirement. We have had the privilege of vacationing in Hawaii, Puerto Rico, Aruba, and the Virgin Islands. We own rental properties and live in a home that we thought would be ten to fifteen years in the future for us. Susan and I are fortunate enough to donate to worthy charities. We have the daily stresses like everyone else, but we do not live in financial fear. My situation today is miles away from my life just seven years ago. I would not consider myself rich. But I am abundant, and I am becoming more abundant by the day.

You Don't Know What You Don't Know

The first step was to open my mind to what I did not know. "You don't know what you don't know" sounds like common sense. This expression is powerful. Many of us stroll through life thinking that we have the answers, but the truth is that most of us do not. That is the worst place to be. When we think we know something, we shut out any new information. However, we have to take a good look at our condition. Chances are you are not doing as well as you could be doing. It is probably because most of us survive in spite of our ignorance.

Warren Buffett, the renowned investor, gave a speech to the MBA students and faculty at my school. He started his speech by giving everyone a multiple choice quiz. The questions seemed pretty easy. They seemed to be basic common knowledge questions regarding a number of different subjects. When he was done asking questions, he revealed the answers. Amazingly, in a hall with hundreds of well read, well educated professors and students, no one got all of the answers correct. In fact, few got more than half of the answers right. His point was simply this: Although you think you know, you really do not know as much as you think you know. Many people think they know a lot more than they do. The simple truth is that there is much we do not know.

> Since we do not know what we do not know, our knowledge is only an assumption.

The first step to wisdom is to know what you don't know. Think about how scary it is that we can operate in this world confident that we have the answers when we really do not. Since we do not know what we do not know, our knowledge is only an assumption.

Some people struggle with personal finances because of lack of discipline and vision, and some struggle due to plain laziness. Most people struggle because of ignorance. They are smart people. They just do not understand personal finances. The jargon and numbers either scare them away or cause them to tune it all out. I encourage you to not be afraid and to not only tune into your personal finances, but to get in the game. Once you learn a few basic principles, your eyes will be open to all kinds of possibilities. When you start to learn, you will at least know what you don't know, and can begin seeking answers. The goal of this book is to give you the knowledge to move toward your dreams. This book will not teach you everything, but you will at least know what you don't know.

If you are locked in a prison cell of financial bondage and feel like you cannot escape, a little knowledge is your key to freedom. I ask that you forget what you think you know for a moment, and embrace the lessons in this book. I am offering you a chance to escape. Open your mind and your heart to accept the key.

Money Flows

Money is not magical. Money is just a tool, and as with any tool, you should understand its purpose and how to use it properly. I was a history major in college. I hated math, and business stuff bored me. I took what I was paid, spent it, and waited for the next paycheck. All of the discussion about stocks, bonds, loans, mortgages, and all of that was intimidating. I had no real urge to learn those things. I was a young man in the Army, and I was more concerned about what my friends and I were doing the next weekend than about any money matters. It all seemed so complicated, and I had no interest in understanding it. A few years later, I began to understand this money thing. The more I learned, the more it made sense to me. As my father said, this money thing is not rocket science, especially if you view it in the right context.

Money is fluid. Money flows like liquid from one place to another. It goes from one hand to another. The world of money at a high level boils down to two points: Pay to hold and hold to pay.

I know that sounds cryptic, so let me explain. If I deposit money in a bank, they pay me interest for the privilege of holding my money. If I invest in a company by buying stock, I am paying to hold their stock. The company will hold the money I invested, and then pay me a portion of their earnings for allowing them to hold my money.

Here is another example. I borrow money from a bank. The bank charges me an interest rate for holding their money. In this case, I am paying to hold their money. When companies take loans, those companies are doing the same thing we do. They are paying for the privilege of holding someone else's money.

Businesses and individuals pay to hold for a variety of reasons. Some businesses borrow money to pay for resources that will help them produce a product or service that another business or individual is willing to buy. Individuals borrow money to buy homes, cars, education, products, and services.

Overall, money is nothing but a resource that is passed back and forth. There are a million terms for the different ways it is done. There are even more terms for the financial instruments used in these transactions, but the concept is the same. You either pay to hold or hold to pay.

The key to accumulating wealth is efficiently using money to maximize the number of people who are paying you. It is that simple. Many people narrowly view money through a one dimensional lens of "salary in and salary out." Often there is more salary going out than coming in. This forces them to pay banks and credit card companies to hold money, which only worsens their financial standing. In this book, I will explain how to maximize these money transactions so you will be getting paid more to hold than you are paying to hold.

Personal Finance Is Not Difficult

Many people often look at personal finance books as they do diet books. How do you know what to believe? Understanding diet information can be confusing because there is so much information out there. Much of the information is wrong and out of context. It seems as though there is a new diet craze every week. As scientific discoveries happen, the approaches change. In the 80s, high carb diets were the thing. Today, everyone is pushing low carb diets. If that isn't confusing enough, there are plenty of diet frauds that are only scheming to get your money. It is like a huge jigsaw puzzle.

Most people struggle to put the pieces together because they can't see the larger picture.

Personal finance is a much different animal. It really is not difficult, and there is no magic to it. There are no fads in personal finance. If anyone proposes any information, you can take out a piece of paper and a pencil, and determine whether the information is accurate or not. New scientific discoveries have no bearing on sound financial principles. Unlike diet information, personal finance is not a mystery. It is a straight-forward discipline that you can master without a business degree. You just need to know how to add and subtract.

By the time you finish this book, you will be armed with the same knowledge that the rich have come to understand. The pieces of the jigsaw puzzle will start to make sense. At that point, you will be able to complete your picture of financial success. As you put the pieces together, you will get a vision for what you can accomplish. But in order to do that, you must get in the game.

You Have to Get in the Game

Frankly, I am sick and tired of seeing America divided between the haves and have-nots. It deeply saddens me that one set of Americans live out their dreams in comfort while the others sit passively on the sidelines. When I was a kid, I watched the older kids play football. I was fascinated by their uniforms. I loved seeing the players engaged in combat and I couldn't wait until I was old enough to play. I felt horrible sitting on the sidelines living my dreams through the players on the field. When I reached the proper age, I reveled in the joy of hitting and being hit on the football field. I loved making decisions as a player that would make the difference between winning and losing.

Unlike football, you do not have to wait until a certain age or, in this case, income level to participate. You can get in the game now. You can make decisions that can be the difference between financial success and failure. Don't sit idly on the sidelines living through other people. Get into the game of financial success today!

I have seen people start companies from nothing and become rich, and I would always think how lucky they were. One day it occurred to me that they were not lucky. These people got in the game. They stopped sitting on the sidelines and decided to take some chances and the chances worked out for them.

> Like any other discipline, you must study, practice, make sound decisions, and be disciplined in order to succeed.

I remember an advertisement that said, "You have to be in it to win it." The slogan couldn't have been truer. You have to get involved! There is no magic wand. You have to see your personal finance as a game that you dedicate yourself to mastering. Like any other discipline, you must study, practice, make sound decisions, and be disciplined in order to succeed.

Finances Are Important

You might be asking, "Why is it important that I master personal finance?" It is important because mastering personal finance can improve your life and the life of those who inherit your money. It is important because being free financially frees you to do the things that you enjoy. It is important because you can put your children through college without being saddled with hundreds of thousands of dollars in debt. It is important because you have the opportunity to create a legacy of abundance for yourself and future generations. Ultimately, it is important because God wants you to be abundant, and He wants you to share your abundance with others.

In order to become abundant, we need to understand personal finance. Learning personal finance is really fun. Trust me. When you understand the basics and start applying them to your life, you will see dramatic improvements in your financial circumstances. Once you start seeing improvements, you will agree that it is fun.

No matter where you stand financially, you have an opportunity to significantly improve your standing over time with discipline and knowledge. Just think about it. You can plan to become financially independent and actually accomplish it! To that end, embracing personal finance is important to getting where you want to be. It is important for the growth and survival of your family. Too many of us waste our resources and live paycheck to paycheck. How can we escape the bonds of employment and bills to seek that higher level of being if we are constantly focused on the financial treadmill? How can we free ourselves to spend quality time with our friends and family if we are preoccupied with our own survival?

God's View of Money

God has blessed us with the ability to earn and prosper. He has empowered us with the ability to manage our blessings well. God wants us to live abundantly and share gratefully. The New Testament makes several references to money and how we should treat it.

In the Book of Matthew, there is a great example of what God has to say about money.

> *Do not store up for yourselves treasures on earth, where moth and rust destroy, and where thieves break in and steal. But store up for yourselves treasures in heaven, where moth and rust do not destroy, and where thieves do not break in and steal. For where your treasure is, there your heart will be also. No one can serve two masters. Either he will hate the one and love the other or he will be devoted to the one and despise the other. You cannot serve both God and Money (Matthew 6:19–21, 24).*

I encourage you to view money as a resource to accomplish an end. Money is not the end-all. However, we cannot disregard money. That would be like a carpenter discarding his hammer or nails. God provides money as a tool to help Christian families accomplish His purpose. It is a tool that helps His church advance Christianity. This tool brings comfort and relief to those in need. Money sends children to college to equip them with the knowledge to live productive lives. Just as the hammer and nail are not the carpenter's masters, money is not our master.

Treasure = Time + Talent

God has placed three resources at our disposal—time, talent, and treasure. Stated as a mathematical equation: Treasure = Time + Talent. *Treasure* in the scope of this book is financial health. But in the larger scope, treasure is a strong, productive, God-fearing family. Treasure is the positive influence that we have on people and institutions that we touch. Our financial health plays an important role in increasing our treasure.

Following the analogy of the mathematical equation, we know that time is fixed. We cannot increase time. Time is a constant. We can only maximize the time we have by learning how to manage our finances, communicate better with our loved ones, and develop good parenting skills. We must work on our talent in the different areas of our lives so we can increase our treasure in tangible items like money and intangible forms like strong, healthy relationships.

Because God has blessed us with free will, we have control over what we decide to do with our talents. We can increase them or sit on them. Every decision we make has a consequence. We make decisions about what to do with our time, talent, and treasure. We are not victims of our society, families, culture, or employers. Most of us are victims of ourselves because we refuse to improve our lives according to God's purpose. The underlying theme of this book is that we can make decisions about our time, treasure, and talent. We can decide to squander these resources, or we can make sound decisions that will multiply our blessings.

Jesus tells the parable of the talents in Matthew 25:14–30. The talents He is speaking of are our resources. In this parable, the master reprimands the servant who did nothing with his resources. Through this Scripture, God is telling us to make the most of what He has blessed us with. We should strive to multiply His blessings. We should not live in fear, guarding our resources. He is encouraging us to use the talent and time we have to increase our treasure for His sake.

I was sitting in on a personal finance workshop at my father's church. One of the instructors, Lynn Holmes-Ross, came up with an ingenious idea. She took money out of her bank account, and put different denominations of cash in individual envelopes and passed it out to each individual in the workshop. She told them the money in the envelope represented the talent they were given. Their job was to multiply the talent and report on their success at the end of the six-week workshop. At the end of the workshop, the class concluded with each person standing up and reporting on what they did with their talent.

> God is telling us that we need to make the most of what He has blessed us with.

It was amazing what people did! One person used the money to buy a meal for homeless people and to minister to them. Another person taught a couple of girls in her Girls and Boys Club how to start their own business selling popsicles, and the children multiplied the money five-fold. One woman used the money to buy a coat for a poor child in her second grade class who didn't have one, and it opened a dialogue about Christ and His family.

After all the money was collected, there was more money than she distributed. Everyone had a story about doing a good deed or making shrewd decisions to multiply that blessing in six weeks.

Several people's lives were touched through this exercise. The money that was returned was given to a charity, which further blessed people in need. Think about it. In six weeks, they multiplied a small gift in different ways that reflected their individual talents and generosity.

Those people took to their task with vigor, and their results were positive. If you approach your resources and talents in the same way everyday, how much could you accomplish? How many people could you bless? How resourceful could you be with the treasure you already have? How could you bless your family and others around you?

> An amazing thing happens when you wrap your mind around being resourceful and making the most of your talents.

An amazing thing happens when you wrap your mind around being resourceful and making the most of your talents. Most people sit on their talent. Why should we have to be challenged through an exercise like the one conducted in the church workshop in order to multiply our talents? We have a mountain of resources that we can share in a number of creative ways to multiply our talents in both tangible and intangible ways. I challenge you to take $50, put yourself on the six-week challenge to multiply those blessings, and see what your results are. Whenever you wrap your mind around a goal, you will find a way to accomplish it.

Jesus makes a point to tell us that we should multiply our resources, but He warns us to not be so focused on money that we lose sight of the reason we have it.

> *Command those who are rich in this present world not to be arrogant nor to put their hope in wealth, which is so uncertain, but to put their hope in God, who richly provides us with everything for our enjoyment. Command them to do good, to be rich in good deeds,*

and to be generous and willing to share. In this way they will lay up treasure for themselves as a firm foundation for the coming age, so that they may take hold of the life that is truly life (1 Timothy 6:17–19).

Paul wrote this letter to Timothy as a mentor, expressing lessons for Timothy to pass on to the fledgling church at Ephesus. These lessons remain true today. We should not be arrogant with our blessings, but recognize that all our blessings come from God. Because God is our provider, we should put our hope in Him. Paul also reinforces our need to be generous in using our resources to do good deeds and help others. He is saying that it is okay to be wealthy as long as we do not focus on our wealth on earth, but strive to create a greater wealth in heaven.

The Bottom Line Is Decision-Making

This book boils down to making wise decisions. The key to financial success is decision-making. Where do I invest my resources? How much do I give? How much do I spend on my needs and wants? Which debts do I pay off first? Just like any game you play, your decisions make the difference between winning and losing.

One of the goals of this book is to educate you, so you can make more informed decisions about your personal finances. As you learn the lessons in this book,

> The key to financial success is decision-making.

think about decisions (good and bad) that you have made in the past. How have those decisions affected you? How could better decisions help you accomplish your dreams? I encourage you to absorb all of these lessons. After you have read this book and put these principles into practice, go out and learn more. This is not astrophysics. Personal finance is about making decisions, and you can make these decisions using simple math. You can free yourself from that prison cell, and this book will be the instruction manual that allows you to plot your escape.

Review

1. You have the resources to free yourself from financial bondage. This book will show you the methods and resources to escape.

2. Understand that you don't know what you don't know. The first step to freedom is to find out what you don't know so you can begin seeking answers. Open your mind to new information and perspectives.

3. Money is fluid. All the talk on CNBC and other financial news shows is about paying to hold or holding to pay. The general concept is that simple: You pay to hold someone else's money or someone pays you to hold your money. If you grasp that concept, the lessons in this book will be clear to you.

4. Get in the game. Do not sit on the sidelines any longer. Get actively involved in controlling your personal finances.

5. Finances are important to accomplishing God's mission, which includes providing security and stability for your family as well as advancing His church.

6. Treasure = Time and Talent. Your treasure is all of your resources—your money, family, and all of the people and organizations you influence. If you maximize your time and talent, the result will be more treasure. No matter what your talent level is, if you maximize your talent, you will have abundance.

7. Everything is about decision making. You are where you are today, by and large, due to decisions you made. Your future results in life have a strong correlation to the decisions you make. I wrote this book to help you take charge of your finances and start making more informed personal finance decisions.

8. These lessons from my father have guided my decisions in all areas of my life, especially with regard to personal finances. I am certain these lessons will help you too.

The LORD gave me this answer: "Write down clearly on tablets what I reveal to you, so that it can be read at a glance. Put it in writing, because it is not yet time for it to come true. But the time is coming quickly, and what I show you will come true. It may seem slow in coming, but wait for it; it will certainly take place, and it will not be delayed (Habakkuk 2:2–3 TEV).

Have a Vision

"The most pathetic person in the world is someone who
has sight, but has no vision."

Helen Keller

One day I called my dad just to talk about sports or anything else that might be of mutual interest. The conversation suddenly went from the typical greeting and small talk, when I was blindsided by a lesson I did not expect.

"So what's going on at work?" Dad asked.

"Nothing much."

"Your mom tells me that the two of you talked the other day, and you said that you did not know what you were going to do or which direction you were going."

"Well, I figure I'll play it by ear. I'm making a good living. I pay my bills. I'm just going to see what the future holds."

I could hear the irritation in Dad's voice as he said, "Son, you aren't eighteen years old."

Now I was irritated. "I know I'm not eighteen years old. I am making a great living, but I don't know what the future holds. So I am playing it by ear."

"Son, there are two types of people in the world: those who act and those who are acted upon. People who have a plan will maneuver and act according to their vision. If you do not have a vision and work to make that vision a reality, you will be the pawn in everyone else's game. Successful people know what they want to accomplish. They have a vision. If you do not have a vision and act according to your plan, people will use you to accomplish theirs. If you are going to win in life, you have to get in the game, and play to win. If you get in the game and stand around with no objective or vision, you will be road kill on the road to other people's success."

> If you do not have a vision and act according to your plan, people will use you to accomplish theirs.

Wow, point taken! I never really viewed life in those terms, but he was absolutely right. I had bought into the theory of being the good corporate soldier. I excelled in my job, but I was working hard because that was my make up. I was not doing it with specific objectives in mind. At the same time, people around me had their agendas. Whether their agendas were corporate success or building contacts for future endeavors, they were in the game and playing to win. On the other hand, I was in the game, but meandering around the field with no set vision. No one was going to come up to me and fulfill my dreams. No one was going to articulate my vision for my family for me. I had to take responsibility and come up with a vision and act accordingly.

That lesson made me think of different people I had met in the past. One guy worked for years for a Fortune 500 company. He aggressively took several different jobs during his time with the company. Was he angling for some big corporate job? No, he was learning all he could while he supported his family. He was learning every facet of the company he worked for so he could start his own company and compete with his current employer. This guy had a vision of running his own successful company. Every day he got up to work hard, not just because it was in his make up as a person. He did it with the vision that within ten years, he would own a successful business.

When the time came, he quit his corporate job. He had the money he needed to start his company. He had his contacts in place and the knowledge he had gained from working in several different positions. With that, he started a wildly successful company that earned him more money than he ever dreamed of making in the corporate world. He also had the freedom to spend time with his young children. This gentleman had a vision. He saw his vision in Technicolor and worked hard for years to make his vision a reality.

Think about some of the obstacles he must have encountered. He had to fight his vanity to take jobs that were not necessarily upward in the corporate food chain. He had to avoid petty squabbles along the way because he had to meet and gain the respect of people who could help him accomplish his vision someday. In some cases, he had to take jobs that paid less in order to acquire the skills he knew he would need to be successful on his own.

I thought about my approach, and I was embarrassed. How could I ever truly reach my potential or accomplish my dreams if I didn't have a vision? All the education and intelligence in the world can't make up for vision. You must have a vision. As a case in point, think about some famous people. How has their vision affected millions of people?

Famous Visions

Martin Luther King, Jr., by all accounts was a quiet, humble, soft-spoken man. He pastored a church in Atlanta at a young age. Suddenly, the social and political climate of the late 50s and early

60s forced Reverend King onto center stage. As the leader of the Civil Rights Movement, he had a vision. He had a vision of a less divided nation. He had a vision of equal opportunity for all men and women. His vision transcended the confines of a black movement to be considered a human rights movement.

His vision was not only about the end result of more equality and greater opportunity for all. His vision also included accomplishing his ends through non-violent means. The Reverend Martin Luther King, Jr. saw decades beyond his death. His vision was a complicated vision of peaceful means and peaceful ends. People during his time could not conceive of equal rights as we know it today. Although everything is not perfect, a humble preacher from Atlanta had a vision. His vision was so powerful, and had so much momentum that even his assassination could not stop it from becoming reality. His vision has shaped American society as we know it today.

The African Methodist Episcopal (A.M.E.) church was the first Christian denomination established by and for persons of African descent. The church was founded on the vision, courage, and leadership of Richard Allen, an ex–slave. Richard Allen had a vision for his life and was willing to work to free himself and his family. Allen reached an agreement with his master on a price for his freedom. After completing his daily tasks for his master, he hired himself out to earn and save enough money to buy his freedom. After purchasing his freedom, he continued working and saving until he was able to secure his brother's freedom. Richard Allen's vision was not limited to personal benefit. When he and other blacks were denied the right to pray and worship in a local church, he led a movement that led to the establishment of the A.M.E. church. Through Allen's vision and legacy, millions of people have been freed. The A.M.E. church is now a global denomination with a membership of more than six million people. Richard Allen was a giant visionary and role model for the ages.

President John F. Kennedy had a vision that changed the modern world. He envisioned America putting a man on the moon before the end of the 60s. Today, it seems like no big deal, but just think about how that must have sounded in May 1961 when Kennedy articulated his vision to Congress. Space travel was something of a fairy tale. There were shows that glorified space travel as some futuristic adventure, but it was not a reality yet. People must have thought that he was crazy. Even if space travel was on the horizon, the idea of putting human beings on the moon and bringing them back to Earth safely was insane.

President Kennedy was serious about landing on the moon, and he made it clear that it was a priority for him. With that vision, scientists raced against the clock to miniaturize electronics. They discovered new materials in the effort to make landing on the moon a reality. They created innovative ways to supply oxygen to humans during space travel—all because of one man's vision.

Kennedy's vision was a Cold War strategy. If we could conquer space, it would give the U.S. a leg up on the Russians in the technology race. It would also help us produce better technology that would ultimately lead to better weapons to deter a nuclear attack by the Russians. Little did Kennedy ever dream that his vision spawned a technological boom that we still benefit from today. And it started with one man's vision.

The apostle Paul had vision. In fact, he is one of history's greatest visionaries. He saw the potential in Christianity. He helped Christianity grow to the massive following it is today by preaching the gospel and writing letters that make up three-fourths of the New Testament. He railed against some of the disciples to change early doctrine to make Christianity more widely accepted by sharing Jesus' message of salvation with non-Jews. He had a divine vision of what Christianity would be, and he focused his energies on spreading the gospel.

Paul's vision guided his actions. His passion for his vision energized Jews and non-Jews. His zeal created the modern church that provides sanctuary and guidance. His efforts have taught legions of people lessons in morality and faith. Modern governments stand on the principles that Paul preached some two thousand years ago. Paul's vision created an organization that has led millions of sinners to salvation.

President Abraham Lincoln had a vision of the United States of America being a truly free society. Before Lincoln, the U.S. was a collection of states. People associated themselves more with the state they were from than their country. Even the military was organized by states. Lincoln's vision thrust the nation into a civil war. He could have compromised his vision. He could have backed down from the South to avoid all the bloodshed and turmoil, but he was resolute in his vision. He had the courage of conviction in his vision to see it through. We can thank Lincoln for the United States we have today. Without his vision, we would not be the free society where so many wish to live.

The ultimate visionary was Jesus Christ. He had a vision for this world that we are still wrestling to understand. He had a vision of peace and forgiveness for every individual. He brought a message of hope and faith. Jesus single-handedly turned the world on its ear. His vision created such a paradigm shift that the world has never been the same since He graced the earth.

Regular Guy Vision

One of the guys in my Toastmaster's club, Doug Keipper, is a regular guy. Doug would gladly admit that he is your average guy. He works in a bank. He has a wife and kids. Doug has a passion for public speaking and NASCAR. So why am I mentioning Doug? Because Doug, the regular guy, has vision!

Doug saw other people investing in real estate and decided to take action. He bought real estate books and learned all he could. Then, he got off the sidelines and got into the game by buying his first rental property. He was by no means an expert, but he decided that there must be other people who were like him, afraid of taking that first step into real estate and not knowing what to do. So Doug decided to write a book, *How to Succeed and Make Money With Your First Rental Home.* He shopped the idea, and to his surprise, a major publisher accepted his book. He has since sold over seven thousand books, and purchased three more rental homes. The following is an excerpt from one of his e-mail newsletters.

I close on my 4th rental house next Friday unless the survey takes longer than proposed. I bought a 2 bedroom, 1 bath 1200 square foot house that needs about $15,000 to $20,000 in repairs. It is a one owner house built in 1957. I paid $60,000 for it and it appraised AFTER repairs for $100,000. This house sits on a 75 x 140 lot with an empty lot next door. I'm hoping I can convince the zoning board to let me build a house on the lot next door since I will now own that free and clear. The house was referred to me by a contractor who has worked on all three of my rental houses and my personal house as well. I have remained motivated by defining this clear goal in my mind and repeating it daily— sometimes 3–4 times a day.

I want to wake up 10 years from now with 20 houses that have $50,000 of equity in each one. That is $1,000,000 in equity. I can then get equity lines of credit and pull that equity out and spend it like income. Cash distributions from loans are not taxable. As long as the properties remain cash flow positive the additional expense from the new loan will be paid by the tenants. If I spend $100,000 per year (equal to $150,000 taxable income) it will take 10 years to spend the million dollars. In that time the houses will continue to escalate in price and the cash out cycle will start over again.

I repeat this daily.[1]

This regular guy has vision. He took the first leap of faith and built upon his initial success. Now he has a full-blown vision of owning twenty rental properties. Not only does his vision include the number of homes he wants to own, but he knows what he wants to do with the equity. This is a perfect example of a regular guy with extraordinary vision. That vision came from getting into the game. That vision came from making an incremental leap. You can do this too!

God's gift to man is vision.

Personal Vision

God's gift to man is vision. Where would we be without it? We all have the capacity for vision. In fact, we all utilize vision on a regular basis. The problem that most people have is applying vision to the broader picture. We know how to have incremental vision, but we are afraid of venturing out to paint a magnificent, colorful picture for our lives. Think about your average day. You have a picture in your mind of what you want to accomplish. If you close your eyes, you can see your chores completed. You can see the items on your to-do list vanishing. I sit at my desk at the beginning of my day and I visualize getting through my voicemail and e-mail. I visualize

---

1. Doug Keipper, e-mail to First Rental House Newsletter mailing list, October 16, 2004.

mowing through my workload and going home with peace of mind. We all have the capacity for vision.

When I was in high school, I ran cross-country. I was far from the most talented runner on the team. One day, I had a great practice, finishing most of the intervals with the better runners. That's when the light came on for me! If I could keep up with these guys in the workouts, why couldn't I be just as good as they were? I took this challenge in incremental steps. I wanted to see if I could repeat my last performance in the next workout. Once again, I kept up with the better runners. Over the summer, I thought about consistently being one of the better runners on my team. It would be a stretch for me, but I had confidence from my small personal victories during a couple of spring workouts.

I made a plan. I was going to improve my running time little by little until I was truly a contender. I put together a summer workout plan for myself. I ran different distances at varying paces. I saw my time decrease little by little. That encouraged me. Those incremental steps allowed me to dream. Why couldn't I be all-state next year? I increased my workouts. I read running magazines constantly to find new ways to improve. The more I worked, the lower my times got over the summer. I allowed myself to dream. I truly believed I could accomplish my goal!

Those incremental personal successes opened my eyes to whole new possibilities. I then wrapped my mind around my goal. I would fall asleep envisioning myself crossing the finish line in the top fifteen, and standing on the stage after the race to receive my award. In the next cross-country season, I finished thirteenth in the state championship race, achieving my goal of being an all-state cross-country runner. When I finished the race in the top fifteen and received my award on stage, it was not foreign to me at all. I had lived that moment a thousand times before that day. The average runner accomplished an otherwise impossible goal through incremental vision.

There is nothing wrong with incremental vision. Sometimes we need to have smaller visions in order to make it through the day. The problem is that many of us cannot envision having a winter and summer home. We can't envision running our own company. We can't envision retiring at age fifty. Why is it that we can't envision a larger vision for ourselves? Much of it is psychological. We subconsciously think that if we paint a grand future for ourselves, we might not achieve it, and we will have to suffer yet another one of life's disappointments.

I challenge you today to paint a grand vision for yourself. What do you have to lose? In fact, you have everything to gain from having a clear vision of your future. Not having a vision for your future is like going on a trip without a destination in mind. Can you imagine jumping in the car with your family to go on vacation and just driving aimlessly? You might enjoy each other's company as you head east, then west, then south, but the bottom line is that you are going nowhere fast.

Let's take a different approach. You wake up one day and decide that you want to take your family to Disney World. That is a starting point. You and your family can envision strolling through the park, enjoying the rides, eating great amusement park food, fraternizing with larger than life characters straight from your childhood books, and wrapping up the night with a spectacular fireworks display. That is an easy picture to paint in your mind.

Now how do you get there? You must have transportation. There is a car in the garage. Great! You must have money for gas, food, and lodging. You save for months for this trip. You have the money necessary. You need to know how to get there. You and your family break out a map and determine which highways to take. You figure out where you might stop and stay for the night if the trip is too long to do in one day. When you have it all figured out, you get the family together one morning and head to Disney World. That wasn't so hard.

That is vision. You envisioned the destination and how wonderful it would be to reach that destination. You saved money in order to make the trip. You made sure you knew how to get there, and you determined how fast you would get to your destination based on the resources available to you.

This vision stuff is not hard. In *The Seven Habits of Highly Effective People,* Stephen Covey states that there are two creations: a mental creation and a physical creation. You must first envision what you want to accomplish before you can make it a reality. If you do not take the time to do that, you will receive whatever life hands you. In essence, your future will be a future of default instead of design.[2] Take time to think about where you want to be financially. Everyone's goal will be different. Some people will dream of running a multi-million dollar business. Others will dream of more limited goals like not having to work after retiring at a particular age. Some dream of having the financial freedom to pursue their dream without being concerned about monthly bills. All of these are valid dreams. These goals may change over time, but you have to start somewhere. The place to start is a strong foundation.

I believe that vision is an indispensable attribute of leaders and successful individuals. Vision is the ability to see what does not exist. Vision is powered by faith. Vision is the aspiration for a set of conditions that when manifested create a new and better world. Whenever a person can see what God sees and commit to sacrifice and work for the fulfillment of the vision, powerful forces move with the person, and great things happen!

Once a vision is committed to, it becomes a strong driver of our thoughts, values, and actions, so we need to be very careful in defining our vision. We need to align our vision with our purpose and God's will. When you have developed and written your vision, you'll see that everything becomes focused on the vision.

---

2. Stephen Covey, *The Seven Habits of Highly Effective People*, New York: Simon & Schuster, 1989, 99–100.

Your real mission is to know what God wants for you. Then you can develop your vision based on aspiration. Vision is always beyond your immediate reach. Vision wakes you up in the middle of the night with a new idea. Vision causes you to meet people with resources and advice to help you move closer to realizing the vision. Without vision, we have little to live for. The Bible says that without vision, people perish (Proverbs 29:18). What's your vision for your financial future?

Where God gives a vision, He provides the provision and marshals all of the necessary resources. All that He requires from us is faithfulness. The only prerequisite for being a good steward is being faithful. Pray for God to write it plainly, and pursue it daily.

Free to Dream

Now, close your eyes and think of a vision for yourself. We will do this exercise in increments. What would you like your financial standing to be one year from today? How about five years? Ten years? Twenty years? Do not bog yourself down with negatives. Be free to dream. Will you be doing what you love five years from today? Will you be financially independent ten years from today? Will you go on mission trips without concern about paying bills? Can your children attend an Ivy League school when the time comes without worrying about how you're going to pay the tuition?

Feel free to dream. Most of us limit ourselves. We see ourselves as only deserving to live in a home of this size or driving a car of that make. We can accomplish anything that our talents can lead us to accomplish. I am a huge sports fan. Wouldn't it be great to own a sports franchise? There is no reason why I cannot accomplish that goal. It may require that I excel at work. It may require me to take some calculated risks and save, but it is not inconceivable. I want you to spend a few moments dreaming.

Many people who have realized their dreams had humble beginnings. Several millionaires sold products door-to-door or waited tables while they worked on their dreams. A young waitress who might have served you at a restaurant may some day own a chain of restaurants and several homes. We can only achieve what we allow ourselves to imagine. Mental pictures are powerful because they have the power to significantly change our lives or even the world. Mental pictures of success can motivate us to take the necessary actions to grow.

A great way to maintain that discipline is to write down your dream in vivid detail. I am encouraging you to think of your dream in detail and describe it on paper. Think about this carefully. Also, think about what you want in the next year, five years from now, ten years from now, and even thirty years from now. Do not be shy in this exercise. Think big. Later on, when we get into investing, you will see how even a goal of $1 million is not far fetched at all. In fact, it is thinking small, especially if you are young.

Take the image of the mental picture you wrote for yourself to the next level by having a visual symbol of the reward to generate discipline. For instance, if you dream of owning a certain type of house, get a picture of that house and display it where you will see it every day to remind yourself of why you are being disciplined. I would even take it a step further. It is important to be able to see the end result of your hard work and discipline. If you dream of owning an expensive sports car, picture the exact color, make and model of that sports car. Take it a step further, and go test drive your dream car. Go with a realtor and walk through that $2 million home and imagine yourself and your family relaxing in that home during Thanksgiving or Christmas. Without a tangible reward, it will be easy to stray away from your well thought out plan.

This is not to say that investing in expensive sports cars is an ideal use of your money. The point of this exercise is not to be materialistic. The point is to get you focused on a goal. At least the picture will be a driving force to exercise financial discipline for your long-term goals.

You Are Not an Island Unto Yourself

I was very fortunate in my timing. God blessed me to find my wife, Susan, and marry her after I got my act together. I learned my lessons and put them into practice. Once I met Susan, it was even more important to me to have my personal finances together so that I could provide a better life for our family. Many people do not have the fortune of learning these lessons and putting them into practice before adding a spouse and kids to the equation.

If you and your spouse are financially undisciplined, it is a recipe for disaster. In that type of relationship, your individual problems are compounded. One of the leading causes of marital strife is money. Even two disciplined spenders have problems combining their personal resources and making spending decisions, so two undisciplined spenders bound together in holy matrimony are a train wreck just waiting to happen.

For married couples, it is important that you make a budget together. It is essential that you create the vision of where you want to be financially together. You must both buy into the vision, and be willing to compromise in order to make it work.

When I got married, I realized quickly that my spending priorities and Susan's were very different. I thought that buying shoes was a waste of hard earned money, and she felt that golf was too expensive and a waste of money. We were both right. However, we had to come to an agreement on the things that we both enjoyed spending money on. We began by developing a new vision of what we wanted to accomplish together as a family. Then, we restructured our budget to accommodate both of our needs and decided what we were willing to forgo in order to enjoy those luxuries, and continue to live within our means.

I am not here to play marriage counselor. Whole books have been written on the subject of marriage and finance. I am simply making you aware of the fact that it is much more difficult for two people to make a budget than one person doing it alone. When you are married, the stakes are higher because they affect your family. This is especially true if you have or plan to have children. If you execute a plan and save money, you will allow your children and grandchildren to begin their financial lives with a head start. Your financial discipline gives you an opportunity to create a legacy.

In order to accomplish anything, you must have vision and be laser focused on accomplishing that vision. If you are focused, you will put the pieces together to paint a vision for yourself and your family. The first step in realizing abundance is the ability to see abundance. Put the book down, and write down your vision. Write a broad vision. Then break it down into incremental goals—one, five, ten, and twenty-year goals.

> If you execute a plan and save money, you will allow your children and grand-children to begin their financial lives with a head start.

For example, you might decide that you want to be free of consumer debt and have $2,000 in your savings account in year one. Five years from now, you might want to own a $250,000 home, be free of consumer debt, and be on the verge of starting your own company. Ten years from now, you may want to own two homes and have a net worth of $500,000 with $50,000 in savings. When you create goals for yourself and put them in writing, your mind automatically wraps itself around those goals, and you start looking for ways of accomplishing them.

The first step in achieving your goals is learning to manage your personal finances. Having goals is great, and the goals look pretty on paper; however, if you do not have the knowledge and discipline to effectively make them a reality, they won't be worth the paper they are written on. The next step is to make incremental leaps.

Incremental Leaps

What are incremental leaps? Incremental leaps are small decisions that, with discipline, will move you toward your vision. Many people think about being millionaires, but they feel in order to accomplish that dream, they will have to inherit money from a long lost uncle or win the lottery. That is not true at all. You can do it all by yourself by making small disciplined steps. Those small steps of discipline will grow into larger steps. As you see your vision becoming more and more of a reality, you will be inspired. You can accomplish anything with inspiration.

So let's assume that there is not a multi-million dollar inheritance with your name on it. Let's also assume that you will not win the lottery. Now that we have that out of the way, let's decide to set aside and invest a small amount of money per day. If I told you that you could be a millionaire by investing $2 per day, would you believe me? A couple of bucks are no huge stretch no matter what your pay is. Even if you make minimum wage, you can find a way to set aside $2 per day. That $2 is what I call an incremental leap. I am not asking you to invest $50 a day. I am not suggesting that take any huge risks—just $2 a day.

> Incremental leaps are small decisions that with discipline will move you toward your vision.

Now that you have decided to take that $2 a day incremental leap, let's look at what can happen. Let's assume you are a twenty-five year old woman. You make a modest income, and you have decided that you will put aside $2 per day. Let's assume that you take those dollars that you set aside and invest them monthly into a mutual fund with a return of 12%. Starting from nothing, that incremental leap will make you a millionaire at sixty-eight years old. In forty-three years, taking that incremental leap of setting aside $2 a day with a 12% return can make you $1 million. Now imagine if you set aside $4 per day with the same rate of return. You will reach $1,000,000 after 38 years. I think you get the picture.

You have to be telling yourself that it can't be that easy. The truth is that it is absolutely that easy. You just have to find a little bit of discipline to do it. Let's go back to your vision. What did you write down for a vision? Do you want to revise that dream now that you know that you can invest $2 a day and become a millionaire in 43 years? Maybe you will consider broadening your vision of success. The incremental steps will turn into medium and large leaps of faith. Since you have to start somewhere, start from a $2 position and let your vision grow from there.

Review

1. Vision is the starting point for all great accomplishments. Pray about your vision. Ask God to help you discern His vision for your life so that your desires will be according to His will.

2. If you are married, pray together. Discuss your individual dreams. Then, with God's help, together create a single financial vision for your family.

3. If you don't have vision, you will just be a pawn in someone else's vision.

4. Famous people who have changed the world did it through vision. If they can change the world, why can't you transform your life with vision?

5. We all have the capacity for vision. We just need to practice it. Practice by having a vision for one day in your life. Then stretch it to a month, a year, and five years.

6. Tap into your own history. Everyone has accomplished something special through personal vision. You just need to identify it and replicate it.

7. Write your vision on paper. Then write down incremental goals for one, five, ten, and twenty years.

8. Make your vision tangible by literally touching and feeling symbols of your vision.

9. Incremental leaps are a powerful way of bringing your vision to reality. Taking small steps will open your eyes to a greater vision, but you have to take the small steps first.

10. God has granted us the power to dream, and He has blessed us with the resources to make His vision for us a reality.

Continuing the Lesson

Study these Scriptures for a deeper understanding of what God says about vision and how to discern His vision for you.

Proverbs 3:5–6

⁵Trust in the LORD with all your heart and lean not on your own understanding; ⁶in all your ways acknowledge him, and he will make your paths straight.

Habakkuk 2:2–3 (TEV)

²The LORD gave me this answer: "Write down clearly on tablets what I reveal to you, so that it can be read at a glance. ³Put it in writing, because it is not yet time for it to come true. But the time is coming quickly, and what I show you will come true. It may seem slow in coming, but wait for it; it will certainly take place, and it will not be delayed.

James 4:13–15

¹³Now listen, you who say, "Today or tomorrow we will go to this or that city, spend a year there, carry on business and make money." ¹⁴Why, you do not even know what will happen tomorrow. What is your life? You are a mist that appears for a little while and then vanishes. ¹⁵Instead, you ought to say, "If it is the Lord's will, we will live and do this or that."

Lesson 2

Give Generously, Yet Wisely

"We make a living by what we get, but we make a life by what we give."

Winston Churchill

"Money is like manure; it's not worth a thing unless it's spread around encouraging young things to grow."

Thornton Wilder

My parents had just returned from celebrating their anniversary in Italy. I stopped by to hear about their trip and catch up on what was going on in their lives. After talking about the high points of the trip and current events, somehow we segued into a personal finance discussion. My father started talking about giving, and I was intrigued by what he had to tell me. My father said very matter-of-factly, "Our financial fortunes changed when we decided to start tithing in 1981."

My dad is a master at throwing out controversial statements to bait me into asking the obvious follow up question.

"What do you mean? How could that possibly be the case?" I asked, curious, but leery of what he was drawing me into.

"When your mom and I became obedient to God with our blessings, He opened up a world of blessings to us that we would not have otherwise realized."

He went on to explain how after he made the commitment to tithing, he was promoted and received the biggest pay increase of his life. My father also said that even though he had made the mistake of living beyond our means, his continuing obedience in the form of tithing sustained us.

He told me that we should give with a free and willing heart. Jesus is the prime example of generosity and charity. He obeyed God from the time of His birth to the moment He died on the cross. God gave us our blessings. The least we could do is tithe.

Then Dad said, "When you go to a restaurant you tip at least fifteen percent, right? What did the waitress do for you besides bring your drinks and food to the table? God provided you with the means to buy that food. Doesn't He deserve at least ten percent?"

"Great point, Dad."

"There are some people who are generous, but they are foolish about how they give. Some people give money to friends and family with no criteria at all for giving. This will create some serious relationship problems with the people you love the most."

My father was right on many different levels. We do give freely to people who are the least deserving. Even worse, we begrudge our tithe to God. It is amazing that society has trained us to pay at least fifteen percent to the person who brings food and drinks from a restaurant's kitchen. Most people would not even debate the merits of that, but will fiercely debate the value of tithing.

It also dawned on me that giving freely is a state of mind. Giving is a state of abundance that opens you up to a world of blessings. When we operate on the basis of scarcity, we circle the wagons. We are constantly on the lookout for someone trying to take what is ours. When we approach life with the attitude of abundance, we are not concerned about making ends meet. We do not worry about someone taking what is ours. When we operate with the attitude of abundance, we know that there will always be enough for all of us.

Society trains us to operate in the scarcity mode. We live in a highly competitive culture. We grow up playing sports. We come up in the school system competing to get into the best colleges. In sports, there can only be one winner. If the other guy wins, we lose. In the competition for college admissions, if the other guy gets accepted, there is one less slot available for me. We are so well trained that we grow up approaching every situation as a zero sum game. Life is not a zero sum game. In most cases, we can create win-win scenarios by being generous. The whole concept of generosity is that we should give without expecting anything in return. The blessing is that when we give generously not expecting anything in return, we often get more than we give.

> The whole concept of generosity is that we should give without expecting anything in return.

Tithing

Tithing is simple obedience to God. In His Word, God tells us that we should cheerfully give Him ten percent of our income. God has blessed us tremendously. For His blessing, He wants us to advance His Word and help others in need by contributing to the church.

Many churches, today, struggle because believers are disobedient to His Word. Think about how many people's lives would be changed if we obeyed God's command to tithe. Think about how many people who do not know Jesus would hear the gospel. Consider how many hungry people would be fed and how many sick and elderly people would be assisted.

When we are free from the shackles of debt, we have a greater capacity to give. This giving touches the lives of a wide range of people. Because of your generosity and cheerful obedience to God, you will be blessed.

The 80/20 rule applies in most churches. This rule says that eighty percent of the donations to church come from twenty percent of the congregation. Imagine if all members in a church's congregation decided to obey God's Word. How much could a well-run church accomplish if everyone was tithing? How many mission trips could be sponsored? How many homeless people could be fed?

The Bible makes several references to tithing in both the New Testament and Old Testament. These references are straight-forward. Tithe means one-tenth. Here are a couple of scriptural references to tithing.

> *There you shall bring your burnt offerings, your sacrifices, your tithes, the contribution of your hand, your votive offerings, your free will offerings, and the first-born of your herd and of your flock. There also you and your households shall eat before the Lord your God, and rejoice in all your undertakings in which the Lord your God has blessed you (Deuteronomy 12:6–7 TEV).*

> *You shall also present an offering to the Lord from your tithes, which you receive from the sons of Israel; and from it you shall give the Lord's offering to Aaron the priest. Out of all your gifts you shall present every offering due to the Lord, from all the best of them, the sacred part from them (Numbers 18:28–29 TEV).*

These scriptures make it crystal clear what God expects from us. The spirit of giving is joyful. Giving is not something we should do grudgingly. God does not bless us grudgingly, so we should not be joyless in our giving. We are called to give the best that we have. Symbolically, the authors of these books are calling on us to give what is sacred, not what is left over. It is the equivalent of giving the first fresh slice of a pizza compared to giving the leftover crusts.

Tithing is a conviction. As we grow in Christ, many of us become convicted. We become convicted by different behaviors in our lives that are implicitly sinful. I became convicted of my need to tithe. I was one of those people who put a couple of singles in the offering basket. When I was feeling particularly generous, I would put a ten or twenty dollar bill in the basket. Eventually, I realized that I was literally tipping waiters more than I was contributing to church. That was wrong. I was giving more to waiters, who in many cases did not even provide good service, more than I was giving God.

Slowly, I began to give more and more. The more I gave, the more I was blessed. I do not think that it was a coincidence that my income grew exponentially when I became more generous with my blessings. My career went in a positive direction. I found myself feeling more financial freedom even when I was giving more.

The government encourages us to donate to churches and other charities. There are tax benefits to tithing. You can write off your contributions to churches and charities as a tax deduction. However, we should not give with the expectation of receiving something in return. Tithing is giving back to God for the blessings He has already given us. Just think of how good God is to us! He finds ways to bless us a second time with prosperity for our obedience with the blessings He has already given us.

Foolish Giving

People often give foolishly. Some people give money to people thinking that it will somehow buy love. Men and women give to love interests thinking that expensive gifts and cash will make the person love them more. Others give money to family members without any criteria.

Giving is a touchy subject with many people. It is a serious responsibility. God has blessed you with money that you either earned through your talent and hard work or received without doing anything at all, just because He loved you. Either way, you must make wise decisions on how to share your resources. Remember, those resources are not entirely yours. God only loaned you the resources that you have to carry out His purpose, so you must take the responsibility of giving seriously. Making those decisions is difficult.

You want to help family and friends, but you can create real problems for yourself if you do not approach these situations wisely. Whenever you make giving decisions, you should pray about it before you give. Next, you should create some criteria or ground rules for giving. Everyone is different, so your criteria may be different from mine, but ultimately it should pass two tests: God's principles and common sense. Ask yourself these questions:

1. Who is receiving this money?
2. Is this a loan or a gift? If it is a loan, can you afford to lose the money if the person never repays it?
3. Will this gift set a dangerous precedent that will cause conflict?
4. Is this gift helping this person help him/herself, or is it making him/her dependent?

Giving is a difficult situation to handle, so let's tackle these questions. The first question is important. No matter whom you are giving to, these questions must be examined. If you are giving money to your parents, it is different than giving it to a second cousin. When the Bible tells us to honor our mother and father (Exodus 20:12), He intended for us to respect them and care for them. Mark 7:11–13 makes it clear that God expects us to provide financial support to our needy parents.

The second question has to be clearly articulated to the recipient. If it is a loan, you must set the ground rules for how the money will be repaid. However, you should never give a personal loan unless you are prepared to never receive the money (Luke 6:34–36).

If you are giving the money as a gift, do not attach any strings to the gift. If you feel that there must be strings attached, you should not be giving that person money. God tells us to give to those who ask (Matthew 5:42), and He expects us to do it willingly, without selfish motives (Luke 6:33).

The third question is one of the most difficult to evaluate. If your giving money creates a standard of behavior or expectations, then you are setting a precedent. You should always be careful when setting precedents. If your giving money causes other issues within the family, then you are setting a dangerous precedent, and should avoid such situations. No amount of money is worth creating family strife.

> No amount of money is worth creating family strife.

Most of us have seen or experienced situations in which family members borrowed money, but never paid it back. The person who loaned the money builds up feelings of hurt, anger, and resentment as he watches the person who borrowed the money buy new cars, clothes, and whatever his heart desires, with no apparent thought of repaying the loan. The situation often changes family relationships, shadows family gatherings, and even creates divisions as people take sides. Again, no amount of money is worth destroying your family. Psalm 133:1 says, *"How good and pleasant it is when brothers live together in unity!"*

Also, if people to whom you are giving money expect that you will continue giving them money whenever they run into issues, you will have a problem on your hands. This leads to the final question. If you think that giving the money will make someone dependent on you, you must not give that person money. More often than not, giving money to family and friends to bail them out of financial trouble creates more problems than it solves. Help others as much as you can, but be sure your help is empowering.

Psalm 37:21 speaks to the fundamental principles of giving and lending. The psalmist advises us to give generously. This assumes that the giving is preceded by prayer and discernment. The psalmist also says that the wicked borrow and fail to repay. Therefore, if I extend loans to people who are unable or unwilling to honor their commitments to repay, I contribute to their downfall by my actions.

Abundance Mentality

There is something called an *abundance mentality*. It is a mindset in which you do not clutch what you have with both hands. You give freely because you know there is more where that came from. Having an abundance mentality is an act of faith. You can have an abundance mentality when you know that God will continue to provide for you. Abundance is a state in which tithing and donating to worthy charities is not a setback, but a plus.

Webster's Dictionary defines *abundance* as "an overflowing fullness; ample sufficiency; great plenty; profusion; copious supply; superfluity; wealth." By definition, abundance is not one-dimensional. The definition brings to mind a cup that is overflowing. A vessel having so much that the contents spill freely on the floor is an appropriate visual of abundance. Abundance is multi-dimensional because it overflows and touches everything around it. By contrast, rich is one-dimensional. Rich means that you have a lot of money in the bank. Rich means that you can afford expensive things. That's it.

God wants us to have abundance. He does not want us to be one-dimensional. He wants us to have an overflowing spirit of generosity and love. He wants us to be filled with mercy and grace.

He wants us to have the financial resources we need to live comfortably and contribute. In all of these aspects, He wants us to be so full of generosity, love, mercy, and grace that it cannot be contained in the confines of our physical bodies. He also wants us to be so financially abundant that our wealth spills over to future generations, churches, and charities.

Abundance is more than a descriptive noun. Abundance is a way of life for those who are obedient to God's will. Abundance comes from learning the lessons of our Heavenly Father and applying them to our daily lives. These lessons are a feast of wisdom that will leave all of us full.

The Circle of Blessings

I have a co-worker whose mother died last year. At the funeral, the minister performed a moving sermon. He talked about all the lives this woman touched. He talked about her faith and her dedication to family. I was genuinely moved.

My co-worker came to the U.S. as a Chinese refugee from Vietnam at the age of ten. She and her family, along with a number of other refugees, risked their lives in a rat infested boat, traveling across the Pacific in order to realize the American dream. After a harrowing journey, they eventually found their way to Atlanta where they decided to settle. A local church in Atlanta provided them with clothes and other necessities through their ministry. They also taught them English and helped find employment for them. Ultimately, my co-worker's mother converted to Christianity. She was active in her church and embraced Jesus.

Twenty-five years later she found her way home. When she died, she left three children and a grandchild. All of her children went to great colleges. They all have excellent jobs, and they are living happy, prosperous lives. She had accomplished her mission on this earth. Her co-workers and family held her in the highest regard, and continually spoke of her strong, humble generosity. The chapel was filled with people whose lives were touched in different ways by this woman.

Tithes and offerings made this story possible. The generosity of Christians allowed this family to live the American dream. In turn, they blessed many people in their community.

Tithing starts the circle of blessings. How many other stories are there like that? How many more amazing stories could there be if we simply decided to be obedient and tithe? The circle of blessings impacted an entire family, their future generations, and all of the people who have come in contact with them. It all started with one congregation putting tithes and offerings in the collection plate.

Giving Freely

If you gain absolutely nothing else from this book, I hope you remember this: God first wants us to love Him and know Him. Not tithing will not keep you from heaven, nor will it deny you God's grace and mercy. However, He says in John 14:15, *"If you love me, you will obey what I command."*

Tithing is an abundant act of giving to God and expecting nothing in return. The essence of giving is that you are doing it freely. I am sure that God does not regret His decision to sacrifice His only Son. How silly is it for us to begrudge God His tithe? Even worse, how awful would it be if you grumbled about giving?

If you do not tithe today, I encourage you to do so. If it is not in your heart to do it today, consider it. The book of Hosea says, *"For I desire mercy, not sacrifice, and acknowledgement of God rather than burnt offerings" (Hosea 6:6).* This Scripture tells us that we should strive to know God and love Him. The more we get to know the Father, the easier it is for us to act obediently by tithing.

If someone sacrificed a loved one to save your life, how grateful would you be? If someone provided you guidance, strength, and wisdom when you needed it most, what would you do for that person? If someone provided you with talent and skill that allowed you to earn a living for yourself and your family, what would that be worth to you? As you grow to know God and appreciate His generosity toward you, tithing will seem like a small sacrifice.

Knowing God and loving God leads to obedience. Obedience will lead to tithing, and tithing will lead to abundance in the material and spiritual. Once you grasp the concept of obedience, the rest of this is easy. The remainder of this book provides you with the knowledge and tools to maximize your blessings, which will make tithing that much easier.

As you learn more about personal finance, remember the importance of being generous. Also, remember the importance of being obedient. You will be blessed for it, and others will be blessed too.

Review

1. Commit to tithing. You will be blessed for it.

2. Give without expecting anything in return.

3. Give wisely. Avoid setting dangerous precedents and damaging relationships because of unwise giving. Sometimes you can hurt people more than help them by giving them money.

4. Establish criteria (not strings) for your giving. Having criteria for your giving sets personal standards that keep you from creating problems for yourself and your family.

5. Develop an abundance mentality. Give generously knowing that there is more where that came from because God will continue to provide for you. Nothing makes you realize how truly blessed you are more than giving.

6. The act of giving truly impacts people's lives, even when it is not apparent to you. Your contributions could be helping a family create a secure home and generations of abundance and success.

7. Get to know God, and giving will be easier.

Continuing the Lesson

Study these Scriptures for a deeper understanding of what God says about these subjects:

Tithing

Malachi 3:10–12

[10]"Bring the whole tithe into the storehouse, that there may be food in my house. Test me in this," says the Lord Almighty, "and see if I will not throw open the floodgates of heaven and pour out so much blessing that you will not have room enough for it. [11]I will prevent pests from devouring your crops, and the vines in your fields will not cast their fruit," says the LORD Almighty. [12]"Then all the nations will call you blessed, for yours will be a delightful land," says the LORD Almighty.

Giving to Others

Psalm 112:5

Good will come to him who is generous and lends freely, who conducts his affairs with justice.

Psalm 112:9

He has scattered abroad his gifts to the poor, his righteousness endures forever; his horn will be lifted high in honor.

Abundance

Luke 6:38

Give, and it will be given to you. A good measure, pressed down, shaken together and running over, will be poured into your lap. For with the measure you use, it will be measured to you."

Lesson 3

Keep Score

"The person who doesn't know where his next dollar is coming from usually doesn't know where his last dollar went."

Unknown Author

My father has an interesting way of explaining complex subjects. He likes to ask open-ended questions that really make me think. One day, I stopped by my parents' house just to visit and share a cup of coffee. The subject went from family, to sports, to business. When the subject turned to my personal finances, the next lesson hit home with me.

"How are your personal finances?" asked Dad.

"I guess they are okay."

"What do you mean by that?"

"I mean that they're okay. I pay my bills, and I am not worried about where my next meal is coming from."

My father, with a smirk on his face retorted sarcastically, "Lofty ambitions, Son."

Angry at his reply, I responded defensively, "Well you know that I have lofty ambitions!"

"Okay. What's the score?"

"What do you mean?"

"We were just talking about the Dallas Cowboys game. Do you know who won?"

Dad knows that I'm an avid Dallas Cowboy fan, so this question was outlandish. "Of course, I know who won," I said, feeling exasperated.

"How do you know who won?"

"I watched the game, and I saw the final score."

"So, what is your score with regard to personal finances? Are you winning or losing?"

I couldn't honestly answer that question. In fact, it was a bit embarrassing that I didn't know the answer. I could give detailed stats on every NFL game that weekend, but I couldn't say what my net worth was. Even more embarrassing, I didn't have a set plan for where I needed to be. Not only was I ignorant of the score, but I didn't have a game plan either.

In the chapter about vision, we discussed taking a trip to Disney World. You must know your destination. You must know by what means you will get there. You have to know the resources required to make that trip a reality. I did not have a firm destination. So using that analogy, I was on the highway going somewhere, but I didn't know where I was going, how far I was from my destination, or what resources I needed to get there. I really needed to set a firm destination, determine where I was, and decide how I was going to get where I wanted to go. I needed a financial scorecard.

Financial Scorecard

Your financial scorecard tells you what you are worth financially. The formula to determine your score is Net Worth = Assets – Debt. In layman's terms, your economic worth is the value of what you have minus what you owe. Your financial scorecard reveals the state of your financial health. You probably visit your doctor for an annual physical. It's a good way to make sure your body is healthy and to detect any problems early before they become catastrophic. The financial scorecard is a checkup of your finances.

In this chapter, we will discuss what net worth means and give you practical advice on how to increase it. We should begin this process with the end in mind. Think hard about what you want to accomplish. Write it down. How much do you want to be worth? How much would your net worth need to be before you have the resources to start that business you always dreamed of? Questions like these will get you to thinking about your goals. Work backward.

Let's say that you have a vision of being completely independent of any employer. You want to be able to start your own business, one that will sustain the lifestyle that you envision. If it requires a net worth of $500,000 in order to make that a reality, you should determine what your net worth is today, and figure out what it will take in savings per month in order to accomplish that goal. This dream is not impossible. Although $500,000 sounds like a tall order, it is within all of our reach. But first you have to understand the financial scorecard and determine what your personal score looks like today. Then, you can determine what you will need to do in order to accomplish your goal.

> Your economic worth is the value of what you have minus what you owe.

We begin assessing your financial health by looking at your assets. An asset is something that you own. Let's look more closely at what counts as assets. Below is a list of items that can figure in your asset value calculation. Assets include:

- Real estate
- Cars and clothes
- Jewelry, appliances, and artwork

- Stocks, bonds, 401(k)s, and mutual funds
- Checking and savings accounts

These are the main assets that most people have. These assets can be split into two categories: *appreciating* and *depreciating* assets. Appreciating assets are those possessions that increase in value over time like real estate, stocks, bonds, and mutual funds. Depreciating assets are possessions that decrease in value over time like cars, clothes, and consumable goods. We will examine both types of assets and discuss how they affect your financial scorecard.

Appreciating Assets

Appreciating assets are the keys to improving your financial health. Homes, stocks, bonds, mutual funds, and 401(k)s fit into this category. The value of appreciating assets can fluctuate, but generally speaking, they will increase in value over time. If we can maximize these possessions, our net worth will increase.

Depreciating Assets

A depreciating asset is something that loses its value after you purchase it. The biggest depreciating asset most people buy is a car. I will discuss the financial implications of purchasing a car in the chapter on investments. Other depreciating assets are stuff. Unless that stuff is an authentic collector's item that increases in value, it is depreciating in value. The furniture in your home, the stereo, television, washer and dryer, clothes, and other items have negligible worth after they leave the store. In my personal scorecard, I do not even account for them in my total net worth equation. How much could you sell your used Armani shirt for? Your appliances and electronic equipment are worth pennies on the dollar that you spent for them.

The rule for depreciating assets is: Be careful of what you spend on depreciating assets. They ultimately hold little or no value. If you pay less for the things you need or want, you will have that much more money to put into appreciating assets. This is not to say that you should not have nice things, but the money you spend on those things should be reasonably proportionate to your income. You need to recognize them for what they are—money spent.

The Value of Knowing Your Net Worth

Most people do not know what their net worth is. We work hard week in and week out, but millions of Americans have negative net worth. The reason is that most people do not know how to keep score. Keeping score is important because it is a way to insure that our actions are in step with our goals. In sports, we keep score so we know how we are doing. If you know you are ahead in a ball game, you take a more conservative approach to protect your lead by reducing your risk. If you are behind, you take calculated risks to score more points. The point is that you would not know what approach to take if you did not know the score. Personal finances are no different. You have to know how you are doing in order to improve. You also need to know how you are doing if you are striving for a particular goal.

> Keeping score is important because it is a way to insure that our actions are in step with our goals.

If you know what your net worth is, then you will think carefully every time you spend money. Before you buy that brand new $1,000 stereo, you will have to ask yourself: Is this purchase in line with my overall financial goals? Would I be happy with a decent radio for $300 and putting the rest of it in a mutual fund to get closer to my goal? Maybe you could do without a stereo or a radio for now, which would give you $1,000 toward your goal.

Really wanting to be financial healthy is crucial to making any of this advice work. You have to either feel a lot of pain and/or envision a prosperous future with no financial worries to be compelled to take action. Some people don't even realize how much financial pain they are experiencing, but most people are acutely aware of their struggles. I have seen grown men and women break down and cry in seminars because they were under so much financial pressure. That financial pressure hurt their relationships with their spouses and put a tremendous amount of strain on their marriages. These men and women would tell stories about creditors calling them and their spouses at work trying to collect on overdue bills. Some people talked about having bad credit because they had so much debt that they could not pay it. These people were not people with small salaries. They were college-educated men and women with high-salary jobs.

> Real wealth comes from living within your means and making sound investments.

Many people have excellent jobs and make great incomes, but they are still in dire financial straits. They live paycheck-to-paycheck. They have a tremendous amount of debt. These people drive luxury cars, wear designer clothes, and live in expensive homes with expensive furniture. On the surface, they look wealthy, but when you look closely at their finances, you quickly realize that they are all show. Real wealth comes from living within your means and making sound investments. Expensive clothes and luxury cars do not count for much more than window dressing. Some of these people, for all their flash, have negative net worth. Living for today will put you in a bind when the first major emergency comes along. Just a couple of months without a paycheck would put these people in serious financial trouble.

The natural question is: How does this happen? How could these well-educated people making well above the median income be in financial distress? There are several reasons for this. Later, I will discuss some of the other reasons for this, but the main reason is that they did not view their financial situation as a net worth equation. Would they be in their current situation if they had asked themselves whether their purchases would increase or decrease their net worth every time they reached for their wallets? I think if they had thought of their financial situation in terms of Net Worth = Assets – Debt, they would have behaved differently. It only takes a few times of realizing that your decisions are negatively affecting your net worth to take positive action to change your behavior.

Another reason these well-educated, high-income people struggle is that many do not understand the concept of delayed gratification. They have money, so they spend it as fast as they get it. These people have a terrible time delaying buying that flat screen television today to invest that money for tomorrow. They lack vision, so they have no plan in place that provides them the incentive to delay gratification. Some psychological studies suggest that the ability to delay gratification as a child is a better predictor of success as an adult than intelligence. Those same habits of delaying gratification often stay with you into adulthood. If you haven't been able to consistently delay gratification, practice delaying gratification and investing now. You will see definitive, positive results.

Offense vs. Defense

Earlier, I encouraged you to get in the game. Like most games, there is offense and defense in the game of personal finance.

> Offense is when earn money and put that money to work for us through investments.

Offense is when we earn money and put that money to work for us through investments. We make money, and then we make decisions on what to do with the money we earn. Of course, we have to spend money on our needs. Then we need to make decisions on our wants. This is the tricky part. We can buy new clothes or we can play aggressive offense by investing and saving money.

Defense is as important as offense. Defense is protecting our money from ourselves and others. We have so many people trying to reach into our pockets. We are bombarded with commercials and images of wealth. Every time we turn on the television or the radio there is some actor or actress trying to reach into our pocket selling us products we do not need. When we do not play successful defense, we end up in debt. That debt hurts our financial scorecard.

Remember the financial scorecard is Net Worth = Assets – Debt. We increase our net worth by using our money to either invest in assets or reduce debt. For instance, investing in mutual funds is a decision that will likely increase your net worth as your investment grows over time. Investing $1,000 today could get you $1,100 at the end of a year with 10% growth. On the flip side, if you invest $1,000 in clothes, you would not be able to sell those clothes for a fraction of their original cost. Let's say after one year, you could sell them for $200. It would be even more disastrous if you used debt to purchase that depreciating asset. Now you own something that is worth considerably less than what you paid, and you are carrying credit card finance charges on it too. With the mutual fund investment, you have $100 more than you started with on day one. With the $1,000 worth of clothes, you lost $800 after one year. If you used debt to make the purchase at 15% interest, after one year, you have paid at least $150 in interest, which nets you a negative $950 as opposed to a positive $100. That is a $1,050 difference between those two decisions. That is the power of appreciating assets versus depreciating assets. The same $1,000 was used, but two very different decisions created two very different outcomes. When we give in to commercials and the hype of materialism, we are spending money that could go toward the asset side of our financial scorecard. When we spend beyond our means, we increase the debt side of our scorecard and reduce our net worth.

In the next chapter, we will look at the foundation for financial success—budgeting.

Review

1. The financial scorecard formula is Net Worth = Assets – Debt.

2. Know your financial situation as well as you know your job, interests, and hobbies. Knowing your financial situation is more important than some of the other activities in which we invest our time and energy.

3. A financial scorecard is a map to get you to your vision. How could you possibly know what decisions to make if you do not know your score in the game?

4. Creating a financial scorecard opens our eyes to what we can accomplish. When we know where we stand, we have a better idea of where we want to go.

5. Play aggressive offense (invest) and defense (eliminate or reduce debt). By investing and retiring debt, you will see your net worth increase exponentially and have a glowing financial scorecard.

Continuing the Lesson

Study these Scriptures to better understand what God says about these topics:

Planning

Luke 14:28–30
[28]"Suppose one of you wants to build a tower. Will he not first sit down and estimate the cost to see if he has enough money to complete it? [29]For if he lays the foundation and is not able to finish it, everyone who sees it will ridicule him, [30]saying, 'This fellow began to build and was not able to finish.

Debt

Proverbs 22:7
The rich rule over the poor, and the borrower is servant to the lender.

Romans 13:7–8
[7]Give everyone what you owe him: If you owe taxes, pay taxes; if revenue, then revenue; if respect, then respect; if honor, then honor. [8]Let no debt remain outstanding, except the continuing debt to love one another, for he who loves his fellowman has fulfilled the law.

Wealth

1 Timothy 6:17–19
[17]Command those who are rich in this present world not to be arrogant nor to put their hope in wealth, which is so uncertain, but to put their hope in God, who richly provides us with everything for our enjoyment. [18]Command them to do good, to be rich in good deeds, and to be generous and willing to share. [19]In this way they

will lay up treasure for themselves as a firm foundation for the coming age, so that they may take hold of the life that is truly life.

Proverbs 3:9–10
[9]Honor the LORD with your wealth, with the first fruits of all your crops; [10]then your barns will be filled to overflowing, and your vats will brim over with new wine.

Lesson 4

Live Below Your Means

"Who is rich? He who rejoiced in his portion."

The Talmud

A few months later, I was visiting my parents. They had just returned from South Africa. My parents actually have that life of freedom that most people only dream about. As we sat down with a cup of coffee after dinner, I asked my dad, "What is the key to prosperity? I work hard. I make decent money, but my net worth is not increasing at the rate I would like."

My dad looked over his cup at me and said, "Son, the only way to prosper is to live below your means. If you can live below your means and invest what you have left wisely, you will have financial success."

"Have you always lived below your means?"

"No, your mom and I made a bunch of mistakes. We bought expensive cars before we really had the means to afford them, and we bought a number of other high-priced items that were not necessary. If we had practiced then what we know now, we would have been even better off today."

"What would you have done differently?"

"Exactly what I said. We would have invested more money, and we would have lived below our means. We always lived as if the next promotion or pay increase was around the corner. We were fortunate that I had continued success in my work for a long time. For twenty-five years, we were blessed that we did not face unemployment because if we had, we could have been in real trouble. When I think of the money we wasted during those years, I realize that if we had done what we know now, we would be even more successful. Son, if you create a budget that includes tithing, and live below your means, you will be abundant."

That sounded too easy. Spend less than I make, and I will be abundant. As easy as it sounds, it requires discipline and sacrifice, especially if you are living beyond your means today. My dad's advice was a simple, but eye-opening revelation. In *The Millionaire Next Door,* the authors spent years studying the habits of the affluent. They discovered that the affluent live well below their means. They do not indulge in non-appreciating assets. They practiced being frugal when they had very little and continued that practice. Why would they abandon a practice that has worked to get them where they are? It is second nature to them to spend far less than they earn. If you ever hope to become affluent, you should also get into the same habit. That habit is developed through budgeting. The Scriptures tell us that a wise man saves, but a foolish man devours all that he has (Proverbs 21:20).

> If you create a budget that includes tithing, and live below your means, you will be abundant.

Discipline and vision come in the form of budgeting. Budgeting is the discipline of living within our means. It forces us to think about our vision for our financial future. You cannot budget without thinking about what you ultimately wish to accomplish. You cannot deny yourself that new big screen television or new car without thinking about why you are making the sacrifice—your vision.

Goals, Goals, Goals

With that said, once again we must begin with the end in mind. Look at your vision and the incremental goals that you wrote down earlier. Now, the question is: How do you accomplish these goals? Whether your goals are grandiose or modest, you should make realistic short-term goals. For instance, decide that you are going to pay off one credit card and invest $2,000 without using any credit over the next twelve months. You may find that you can exceed your goal. You may fall a little short of your goal, but the important thing is that you are moving in the right direction. Continue to set goals for one year, five years, ten years, and twenty years into the future. Regularly evaluate where you are and update your goals. Begin with the end in mind, and discipline yourself to that end.

In the short term, you need to set yourself up for success. If you are trying to lose weight, you can dream of losing fifty pounds, but in the short term you need to set realistic goals in order to encourage yourself to the ultimate goal. The idea is to take baby steps. If you decided that you were going to lose ten pounds per week, you might just lose that ten pounds in one week, but the physical and psychological stress would more than likely cause you to binge later or stop working out. Eventually you will feel that your goal is completely unattainable and quit. Then, you end up worse off than you started.

Write down your short-term goals on paper. Look at your goals weekly, even daily, to make sure that you are taking steps every day to accomplish them. There is power in seeing your goals on paper. The act of writing helps you imagine those goals coming to fruition. As you write, think about coming home to your dream house. Imagine running your own business. Imagine your children graduating from college debt free. Feel the ocean breeze blowing across your face as you stand on the back porch of your beach home. See yourself writing a check to your favorite charity. See yourself cheerfully paying your tithe.

Now that you have your goals firmly imprinted on your mind, let's roll up our sleeves and take the first baby steps toward that dream by budgeting.

Budgeting requires discipline. On television, we see people who become wealthy overnight. It happens less frequently than people being struck by lightning. The vast majority of the time, wealth is built over time. When we see successful people, we have to realize that most of them have saved for years and lived well below their means. The truth is: Most people who build wealth in America are hard working, thrifty, and not at all glamorous.[3] They invested well and took calculated gambles with their hard earned money. Many of these wealthy people ran their own businesses and worked long hours for several years to make their businesses successful.

I love to watch Tiger Woods on the golf course. We see him hit the ball effortlessly time after time as the whole world watches him make incredible shots. We see the focus he has on the golf course. What we don't see is the years and years of preparation. We do not see the hours he spends hitting every conceivable shot hundreds of times a day. We do not see him practicing putt after putt as if each one was the winning putt of the Masters.

Likewise, we see wealthy people make large sums of money. We see their lavish homes on television and hear about their new ventures. What we do not see is the discipline in their spending. We do not see the long hours they worked over several years to make their businesses successful. We do not see them early in their careers driving the economy car and clipping coupons while they saved every possible penny to invest in their future businesses. We need to

---

3. Stanley, Thomas J. and William D. Danko, *The Millionaire Next Door.* (Atlanta: Longstreet Press, 1996), 29.

become the Tiger Woods of our personal finances. We need to practice and develop our wealth over time with discipline. In *The Millionaire Next Door,* the authors state that allocating time and money in the pursuit of looking superior often has a predictable outcome: inferior economic achievement.[4] The first step in achieving prosperity is to put away those images of the rich and famous. The proven way to gain prosperity is by gaining control over our spending through budgeting.

> The proven way to gain prosperity is by gaining control over our spending through budgeting.

Assess your financial situation, and then make it a point to save and invest an additional $100 per month. If your net worth equals negative $2,000, a decent short-term goal is to be even within a year. Be free to dream, but be practical in the early, short-term goals you set for yourself. Success breeds success, so set your goals within your grasp.

Budget Mechanics

The formula for budgeting is:

$$\text{Budget} = \text{Income} - \text{Planned Spending} + \text{Savings}$$

You must spend less than you make. That sounds simple, but many people (including myself) struggle with this concept. Although it seems elementary in theory, it is difficult in practice. It requires living a lifestyle that is probably below the one you are currently living. There are few things harder to do than going backward in lifestyle. However, if you ever hope to have a life of abundance, it is necessary to live below your means.

---

4. Ibid. p. 28.

Journal Entries

Habits are created by repeating an action over time. If exercising is a habit, it became a habit over months and years of working out. Budgeting is the second habit you need to learn in order to be abundant. My first step in learning the habit of budgeting was getting my arms around where I spent my money. I bought a little ledger that I took with me everywhere. Whenever I spent any money, I wrote down what the item was and the amount I paid. A few things happened when I started doing this. First, I knew where my money was going and how much I was spending. Secondly, writing down every purchase made me think about my spending constantly. I found myself questioning whether the purchase was necessary. I even felt guilty on days it seemed I was writing too many entries. That exercise really helped me see my spending habits like never before. I could not write down my expenditures without thinking about my goals, and whether that purchase was getting me closer or farther away from my goal.

Before I started writing in the journal, I was not honest with myself about the money I spent. Can you imagine lying to yourself? There were items that I intentionally did not count. It was pure denial. Whether I counted those items or not, they still came out of my bank account. If you are going to accomplish your goals, you will have to face the facts about where your money goes. It is difficult to admit that you spend $100 per month on cigarettes. If you admit that to yourself, you should be compelled to do something about it. Few people will admit to vices, let alone take action to quit or limit them in order to achieve their financial goals.

Budgeting Benchmarks

If you have not budgeted before, it can be challenging. How do you know how much you should be budgeting in each category, e.g., home, food, insurance, etc.? The chart below is a guideline for budgeting. It shows how much you should be spending in each area. Everyone's needs are different, so keep in mind that this is just a guideline. However, it can be a very useful tool when you are taking your first steps into budgeting.

Take out your journal. Add the expenses for each category. If some of the categories are severely skewed, you will need to ask yourself some hard questions. Am I paying too much for products and services in this category? Am I spending too much on clothes? Am I eating out way too often? Am I driving more car than I can afford? These questions are difficult because knowing the answer should compel you to take corrective action.

Budget Guideline Based on $45,000 Annual Salary

Item	Amount	% of Gross Income
Gross Monthly Income	$ 3,750.00	100%
Tithe	375.00	10%
Tax	937.50	25%
Net Spendable Income	2,437.50	100%
Monthly Expenses		
Housing	731.25	30%
Food	292.50	12%
Auto	292.50	12%
Insurance	121.88	5%
Debts	195.00	8%
Entertainment/Recreation	121.88	5%
Clothing	97.50	4%
Savings	121.88	5%
Medical	97.50	4%
Miscellaneous	121.88	5%
Investments	243.75	10%
Total Monthly Expenses	$ 2,437.50	100%

The budgeting guideline is based on a single person making $45,000 per year. I suggest that you take this guideline and insert your income, and see how the numbers look. Are you anywhere close to these numbers? When I did this, my attention was immediately directed to my debts. My percentage for debt was higher, but I rarely bought clothes, so the clothing dollars fell into the debt column. I am rarely sick, so I spend very little on medical care. Therefore, I spread those dollars in other categories. The point is that it doesn't matter so much that your budget fits neatly into these discrete categories. The important thing is that you identify what you make, and determine where you will spend those dollars to stay within your means. The guideline is a great way of framing your budget to give you a starting point.

Budgeting Mistakes

I had tried budgeting before, but my attempts were unsuccessful until I started writing down all my expenditures. The biggest mistake I made was not being disciplined enough to stay on a budget. From a mechanics standpoint, I made the mistake of not being more discrete about my categories. The miscellaneous category consumed a large part of my early budgets because I was too lazy to create real classifications for those expenses. It was also my way of avoiding the truth, so I just shoved the expenses that I did not want to admit to under the harmless umbrella of miscellaneous. Another error I made was to lump all utilities into one category. The problem with lumping the utilities together is that it makes it more difficult to monitor what you are spending on the individual bills. For instance, I used to budget $400 for utilities. This included phone, water, gas, cable TV, and electricity. If my utilities fell within that range, I would continue on happily. However, if I took a closer look at my individual bills, I could scrutinize them in more detail to find ways to save more money.

There are common categories to use for budgeting such as tithing, rent/mortgage, telephone, gas, electric, entertainment, cable, food, clothing, and others. But do not let that limit you. Feel free to create categories that are specific to you. Make sure that the categories are relevant and that you are honest about your expenses. The act of budgeting alone is a great start because it forces you to think about your income and your expenses.

Make your budget work for you. Your budget is a tool, and like any other tool you are in control. Your budget must be flexible because life is all about changes, so your budget should be built for change. The key to successful budgeting is effectively managing the change within your budget.

My Adventures in Budgeting

When I determined that I needed to create a budget, it was a major paradigm shift for me. I had always lived as if I made 10–15% more than I did. Budgeting was a rude awakening, and there were some things that stood out to me. I must confess that, in some cases, I did not take the advice I am giving you, but it was a start. I will walk you through my early budget process and demonstrate areas where I could have saved.

In 1997, my gross pay was $3,750 per month, and my monthly take-home pay was $2,700 after taxes. My original monthly expenses are shown in the following table.

Monthly Expenses

Item	Amount	% of Gross Income
Payroll Taxes	$ 1,050.00	28%
Rent	600.00	16%
Mutual Funds	100.00	2.7%
Car Payment	250.00	6.7%
Utilities	200.00	5.3%
Grocery	350.00	9.3%
Meals Out	125.00	3.3%
Gas	100.00	2.7%
Insurance (Car and Renter's)	150.00	4%
Entertainment	200.00	5.3%
Church (Offering)	50.00	1.3%
Credit Card Payments	400.00	10.7%
Premium Cable	80.00	2.1%
Telephone	150.00	4%
Cell Phone	55.00	1.5%
Miscellaneous	150.00	4%
Total Monthly Expenses	$ 4,010.00	106.9%

My expenses were $260 more than my income, and I did not even come close to tithing. As you can see I did not build in any savings for non-monthly expenses like quarterly insurance payments, car repair, vacation, emergencies, and clothing. Also, I was giving God less than two percent of my take home income. I was living far beyond my means.

I decided to tackle this budgeting project head on to get my expenses in line with my income. First, I set aside $375 for tithing. The rent of $600 would not change until my lease was up. This made the total of fixed expenses at this point $975.

I reviewed my car insurance policy. After looking over the policy, I called the insurance company and went through my options. I realized that my deductible was too low, so I raised it to $1,000, which saved me $30 per month.

I started using regular unleaded at the pump, which saved me $.15 per gallon. It doesn't sound like much, but it saved me $15 per month in gas.

I decided to audit my utility bills. I set my thermostat to 75 degrees instead of 70 degrees in the summer. I also made a point of turning off lights in my home that were not in use. To my surprise, these small actions reduced my electric bill by $35 per month. I discovered that I had a choice of gas providers and switched to a low-cost provider, saving $25 per month. By taking some minor initiatives, I reduced my utilities by $60 per month.

The next bill I took action on was my cable television. I had the premium package with all of the movie channels. I could not remember when I actually sat through an entire movie on television. Most of my television viewing was limited to channels that were included in the basic package, so I changed my plan to basic cable, saving another $50. I find it amazing how people in financial difficulty will find a way to have premium cable or satellite television. I will drive through low-income housing developments and see dozens of satellite dishes hanging off of balconies. Wouldn't you agree that something is wrong with that picture?

My credit card payments were high. I never paid close attention to the interest rate on my credit cards. When I first applied for them, the rates were low. Now, those low interest rate cards were charging me a fortune for the privilege of carrying my debt. I called a credible lender, my bank, and asked about a debt consolidation loan. They offered to combine my total credit card debt into one loan at half the interest rate I was paying on the credit cards. My new monthly payment was $270, and I made more of a dent in my consumer debt than I had before. That was a savings of $130 per month. (Warning: Consolidation loans are a wise way to reduce your monthly interest payments as long as you do not use the added credit capacity to run up more debt on your credit cards. If you decide to consolidate your debt, cancel the cards from which you transferred debt.)

I spent entirely too much on eating out and entertainment. I would go out with friends and pick up their checks. Some months, I went out three times a week. I also ordered expensive take-out rather than making dinner at home. Much of the food in my refrigerator went bad because, in spite of my good intentions, I still ate out most of the time. I tipped big because I didn't want total strangers to perceive me as being a cheapskate. All of this amounted to wasting my hard-earned money just to block my arteries with fattening food.

As a single male, I was not going to stay home in front of the television to save a few dollars, but I did start to become more aware of my spending habits and decided to cut down. I made it a point to stop picking up checks and limited my spending when I did go out. I would order water instead of spending $2 for a soda. I stopped buying appetizers and desserts. All of this saved $45 on dining out and $80 on entertainment.

Groceries were the next target on my list. I generally grabbed whatever interested me as I walked through the grocery store. I would go grocery shopping three times a month and not get much for my dollar. Dining out was a quicker, easier solution to eating, so much of the food I bought went to waste. I started planning my grocery trips. I went grocery shopping when I was not hungry to avoid impulse purchases. I even got the coupon card that saved me as much as $20 per visit to the grocery store. I reduced my grocery bill by $90 per month.

My phone bill needed some work also. Between my cell phone and home phone, I was spending $205 per month. That was way too much. I called around to find the best long distance and local rates. I then changed my cell phone plan to get unlimited night and weekend minutes. To my surprise, the rate for this offer was less than what I had been paying for a plan with fewer minutes. This allowed me to make the majority of my long distance calls to friends and relatives for free instead of burning dollars on long distance. My phone bill went down to $30 per month, and my new cell phone plan with unlimited minutes cost me $50. I saved $125 overall on my phone expenses.

My infamous miscellaneous expenses were difficult to pin down until I started using my journal. They amounted to everything from packs of gum to newspapers and office supplies. There will always be miscellaneous expenses, but they can be limited. Instead of buying a newspaper every day, I decided to read the news online. I stopped making impulse purchases at the cash register. Making small adjustments to my lifestyle saved me $50 per month. Here's what my new budget looked like:

New Budgeted Monthly Expenses

Item	Amount	% of Gross Income
Paroll Taxes	$ 1,050.00	28%
Rent	600.00	16%
Mutual Fund	100.00	2.7%
Car Payment	250.00	6.7%
Utilities	140.00	3.7%
Grocery	260.00	6.9%
Meals Out	80.00	2.1%
Gas	85.00	2.3%
Insurance (Car and Renter's)	120.00	3.2%
Entertainment	120.00	3.2%
Church (Tithe)	375.00	10%
Consolidation Loan	270.00	7.2%
Cable	30.00	1%
Telephone	30.00	1%
Cell Phone	50.00	1.3%
Miscellaneous	100.00	2.7%
Total Monthly Expenses	$ 3,660.00	98%

This new budget was a good start. I identified places where I could save money and took action. Now, I was spending within my means and still had $90 to spare after meeting all of my needs and being obedient to God by tithing. The irony in all of this is that I procrastinated about budgeting, but the minor adjustments that I made did not significantly impact my lifestyle. Much of my money was being wasted through lack of due diligence.

The $90 that I had left over every month went into a savings account to start building funds for other expenses such as special occasions and emergencies. As I started to get my financial life in order, I was motivated to look for ways to cut more expenses out of my budget. Soon enough, I began to see my debt go down and my investments increase.

Eventually, I earned promotions and pay raises. Through the promotions and pay raises, I maintained the same lifestyle and put more money toward ridding myself of debt and increasing my investments. Many people spend their raises and bonuses before they even have them. I encourage you to fight the temptation to spend your additional income. Take that money and apply it aggressively toward your vision.

Within two years, I actually had my spending well under control. I had a savings account that allowed me to vacation and pay for emergencies without climbing back into debt. It took some time to get to this point, and I was also fortunate not to encounter any major personal catastrophes during that time. There were times when I would fall back into my old habits. I made mistakes along the way, but I was dedicated to making my long-term vision of financial security a reality. So, if I faltered, I did not quit. I just got back on track and pressed forward toward my vision.

When I started, I had no specific goals. I just hated that nauseating feeling every month when I paid my bills and realized that I was barely getting by despite a decent salary. Budgeting, like any other discipline, is a growing exercise. It takes time and patience to do it well until it becomes a habit. It might take a few months before your thoughts and actions become one. Old habits are hard to break, and new habits are difficult to start. I encourage you to be patient with yourself and continually work to get your budget in line.

Pay Me Now or Pay Me Later

My budget in 1997 was not ridiculously out of line for a single male in his mid-20s. I invested a lot of money in the consumption of food and entertainment, but that was not what was keeping me down. I reviewed my budget over and over again. It took me some time to realize why, after all my efforts, I only had $15 to save every month. Then, it became clear to me. I was paying for my past sins!

Look back at my budget. The largest expense next to my rent was my credit card debt. My budget was being weighed down heavily by that $270 expense. Imagine if I had that much more money to invest per month. Most of that debt came from bad choices and years of undisciplined spending. I would spend years paying off that debt, when the same money could have had me well on my way to financial security. That consumer debt was nothing more than a claim on my future earnings. MasterCard and Visa owned a share of my future earnings because I spent years consuming more than I earned.

Do you remember the challenge to save $2 a day or $60 per month? If that money was put in a mutual fund with a 12% return, you would earn a million dollars in forty-three years starting from $0. If I could invest that $270 instead of paying debt in addition to the $100 I had been investing, I would have a million dollars in twenty-eight years. Investing $100 per month, I would earn one million dollars in thirty-nine years. It would take me eleven years longer to reach the same goal. All of the nonsense purchases I made to get myself into debt cost me eleven years of financial security.

We make hundreds of choices everyday, and we are rewarded or penalized for our decisions. Before I became sick of getting nowhere fast and started budgeting, I consistently made bad spending decisions that I had to pay for. In retrospect, I would have gladly paid in discipline and knowledge earlier so I would not have to endure the long hike back to financial stability. You have a choice today. I hope that you decide to pay in discipline now rather than in years of wasted money and financial struggle. Later in the book, I discuss asset management and demonstrate the power of investing. In that chapter, you will see the impact of bad decisions and paying off toxic debt in real numbers.

> Financial health cannot be accomplished without discipline around spending, no matter how much money you make.

Financial health cannot be accomplished without discipline around spending, no matter how much money you make. How many millionaire musicians, athletes, and actors have you heard about in the news filing for bankruptcy? Do you think it was because they did not make enough money? Of course, they made enough money. They did not manage their blessings well. They lived beyond their means despite having enormous incomes. They did not have a plan. I would bet that they did not budget. A simple budget goes a long way toward overall financial health whether you are a movie star or a construction worker. In *Unlimited Power,* Anthony Robbins says, "the path to success consists of knowing your outcome, taking action, knowing what results you're getting, and having the flexibility to change until you're successful."[5] Budgeting allows you to think about the outcome you wish to achieve, take action where necessary, know what your results are, and be flexible enough to change until you accomplish your goals.

---

5 Robbins, Anthony. *Unlimited Power.* (New York: Fawcett Columbine, 1986), 69.

Commit to making a budget. The rest of the advice in this book will be of little help to you otherwise. Start and complete your journey to abundance with the discipline and vision that budgeting requires. You will find that the rest of your financial picture will fall nicely into place once you master budgeting.

Now that we have budgeting down, let's go on the offensive by adding to the asset part of our financial scorecard and getting our money working for us.

Review

1. Live below your means. You can only live on borrowed money for so long until you have to pay the price.

2. Budget = Income − Planned Spending + Savings.

3. Commit to making a budget and following it.

4. Get a journal and write down all of your expenditures. It will open your eyes to how much you spend and what you spend it on. It will also prevent you from spending.

5. Find ways to reduce your expenses in all areas.

6. You can pay me now or pay me later. There is an opportunity cost to living beyond your means. Your decision to live beyond your means will cost you several years of your financial life.

Continuing the Lesson

Study these Scriptures to learn what God says about budgeting and debt:

Saving

Proverbs 30:25
Ants are creatures of little strength, yet they store up their food in the summer.

Proverbs 6:6–8
[6]Go to the ant, you sluggard; consider its ways and be wise! [7]It has no commander, no overseer or ruler, [8]yet it stores its provisions in summer and gathers its food at harvest.

Sacrifice

Proverbs 10:4–5
[4]Lazy hands make a man poor, but diligent hands bring wealth. [5]He who gathers crops in summer is a wise son, but he who sleeps during harvest is a disgraceful son.

Discipline

Proverbs 21:5
The plans of the diligent lead to profit as surely as haste leads to poverty.

Lesson 5

Invest, Invest, Invest!

"Investing is simple, but not easy."

Warren Buffet

I started getting my financial life back on track. I got my first big commission check, and at the same time, I received a statement that showed me how well my investments were doing. I was excited, and I couldn't wait to talk to my dad about my good fortune. One day during my lunch break, I stopped by my parents' house. My dad was just pulling into the driveway from a morning round of golf.

"Dad, my investments are really doing well, and I just found out that I will get a nice commission check that will allow me to invest even more."

"The power of investing is amazing! If you invest a little every month, you will be rich by the time you reach middle age," said Dad.

"What has made you so passionate about investing?"

"I grew up without much. My mom worked hard to provide for me, but she was just making ends meet. I didn't know how my life would turn out, but I knew that I wanted something else for you."

"So, you thought that investing would be that something else?"

"I think that investing has ended the cycle of poverty for our family, and investing will elevate you and your family to a better place than we were as a family. My high school principal used to tell me that the measure of success is that you do better than your daddy did. Investing will make you a success, and put you on the road to doing better than your daddy."

My father always told me to "invest, invest, invest." Before he even understood the real power of investing, my father was operating off of the wisdom of common sense. In the early 1980s, my father got into investing in mutual funds. He loved the concept so much that he got his license to sell mutual funds as a side job. The power of investing really opened his eyes and gave the whole idea of "invest, invest, invest" a significant tangible meaning. From my dad's perspective, investing would end the cycle of poverty in our family.

What Does Investing Mean?

Investing is simply making a purchase. Any purchase you make is an investment. You decide whether that investment is worth the cost or not. You decide whether to invest in items that will increase in value or decrease in value. When my father said, "Invest, invest, invest," he meant purchase things that go up in value. In the previous chapter on budgeting, we discussed investing your monthly surplus dollars. The point here is to invest those surplus dollars in something that will increase in value.

> Investing is simply making a purchase... You decide whether to invest in items that will increase in value or decrease in value.

Consider the financial scorecard. Remember, the formula is Net Worth = Assets – Debt. Investing is adding to the asset portion of the equation, which will increase your net worth. You want to acquire assets to increase your net worth. Investments are simply items that you own that have value. If you sell everything that you own, the money you would receive is the value of your assets.

Let's first look at investing in 401(k)s and other financial tools like stocks and mutual funds.

Financial Investing

You should always set aside money to invest in your budget. Investing in appreciating assets will earn money for you and increase your net worth over time. If you are not investing, you are standing still financially. As you learn more about various investment tools, you will see the power of investing, and it will be clear to you how important it is to invest.

> You should always set aside money to invest in your budget.

There are several different instruments for investing. It can be confusing at first, but once you understand the basics, the power of investing will be clear to you. I will provide a brief description of these main investment tools.

Stocks

Stocks are small pieces of a company. When you own a share of stock from XYZ, Inc., you own a tiny piece of XYZ. As XYZ prospers, you will share in that prosperity in proportion to the amount you own. The demand for XYZ's stock determines how much your share is worth. This stock will pay dividends, which are earnings that the company pays to investors for each share of stock they own. Additionally, when XYZ's stock increases in value, the amount of increase is considered a capital gain. That capital gain is yours too.

Let's say that you purchase one share of XYZ for $10. That one share amounts to 1% of ownership in XYZ. One year later, XYZ determines that they made a net profit of $100 that they will distribute to their shareholders as a dividend. You will receive 1% of the $100 profit, a $1 dividend. Later you decide to sell your share of XYZ. XYZ is a popular company now, and their stock is worth $15 per share at the time you sell it. You will profit $5 from the sale of your stock. That $5 is capital gain.

You can invest in stock by contacting a stockbroker or setting up an E*Trade or Ameritrade account. I would not recommend this to a novice investor. Making informed stock decisions requires a lot of homework. Acting on stock tips or guess work is a risky proposition. Sites such as www.etrade.com, www.fidelity.com, and www.vanguard.com are great sources of information about financial markets. You do not have to have a master of business degree to understand the basic fundamentals of investing. These sources not only educate investors, they also allow you to set up hypothetical portfolios to help you estimate the potential risks and rewards.

Mutual Funds

Mutual funds are a collection of individual stocks. Mutual fund companies typically have different mutual funds to offer to consumers. The different funds are set up to focus on discrete categories as broad as domestic and international, or as specific as technology or consumer products. Financial experts research companies in these categories, and then buy and sell large volumes of stock. Unlike stock, you can purchase portions of mutual fund shares. Mutual funds are designed for the common investor who wants to make consistent monthly investments. Just like stock, there is some risk, but the risk is spread out over several stocks in the mutual fund's portfolio.

Mutual funds are a great way to diversify, meaning that you spread your risk across several stocks as opposed to picking individual stocks. If you want to establish a portfolio based on where the whole stock market or specific sectors of the market will go, you can buy index funds that represent all the companies in a particular sector of the market. Some of the more popular indexes of Exchange Traded Funds (ETF) are Standard and Poor's (S&P) 500 and the Dow Jones Industrial Average.

You can invest in any mutual fund by calling a mutual fund company's toll free number and setting up an account. You can make investment arrangements that automatically invest a set amount every month from your checking account. This method of investing helps the investor overcome the psychological hurdle of writing a check every month and makes investing a habit.

Bonds

Bonds are generally safe, low-interest investment vehicles. They are IOUs that companies and government entities use to raise money. The government has ongoing expenses that may exceed the flow of money coming in through tax revenue. Therefore, they offer us an opportunity to make interest on our money by allowing them to borrow the money over some period of time. They pay interest over time depending on the credit worthiness of the borrowing institution and interest rates. Bonds from companies are generally more risky than government bonds since businesses are more likely to have credit problems. The borrower will pay a stated interest on the loan during the life of the bond, and the borrower will also pay the face value of the bond when it reaches maturity. The higher the risk of the bond, the more you stand to gain. Thus, on riskier bonds you stand to make larger gains. That is why government bonds pay relatively low returns.

Bonds are like loaning money to institutions. Let's say that these institutions are friends. The reliable friend has demonstrated that he is trustworthy. His credit is excellent. He has a great job, and he has plenty of ways to pay you back. In the bond world, that company would offer you a low interest rate on the bond because the risk is low. If you were to loan money to the friend who has spotty credit and an inconsistent work history, you would potentially ask for a larger rate of return on that loan because there is a much bigger risk of your friend defaulting on the loan, so he would have to offer you a greater return to convince you to make the loan. Companies and government entities are no different. Purchasing a bond from a risky institution gets you a greater rate of return than purchasing a bond from a safer institution.

Savings and Checking Accounts

Savings and checking accounts are like piggybanks that make money for you. These accounts generally carry very low returns. They are transaction vehicles. Banks pay you for the privilege of holding your money. These accounts are utility accounts.

Your savings account should be used as a lockbox to store cash for an emergency. The amount of the emergency cash needed differs depending on your situation. No matter what your financial situation is, you should have an account that you do not touch unless there is an emergency. The savings account is a great place to put the money that you are saving for vacations, emergencies, Christmas and birthday gifts, car repairs, home repairs, and other situations that you know will occur.

The savings account is a tool that should be used in conjunction with your budget. You have planned for certain events like replacement tires, vacation, gifts, and roof repairs. You have determined that the cost of these items will be $2,400. You should have a line item in your budget for $200 that you place in your savings account every month in anticipation of these situations.

The checking account is another utility account that you use to write checks to pay bills. Make sure that you have some type of overdraft protection in case you make a mistake. Banks offer a line of credit for overdraft. This line of credit, like a credit card, charges you an interest rate for using it. Be careful with this. Many people are liberal in dipping into this credit line. If you must dip into the line of credit, pay it off immediately, and get back on track with your budget.

401(k)s and 403(b)s

401(k)s and 403(b)s are great tools for the average investor. Participation is simple, and most companies offer them. Many employers offer to match some portion of their employees' investment as a benefit to their employees. Additionally, any pre-tax contribution reduces the amount of your taxable income, which saves you money on taxes. You can save on taxes and your employers will match a portion of your 401(k)s investment. Government and non-profit employees can take advantage of a similar plan called 403(b)s. These investments are great deals!

401(k)s and 403(b)s are long-term investments. There is a penalty for removing funds from your 401(k) or 403(b) before you reach 59 ½ years old. These investments consist of any number of tools such as stocks, bonds, and mutual funds. Most plans allow you to choose which type of investment vehicle(s) you want to make up your 401(k)/403(b)portfolio. You can pick mutual funds, stocks, or bonds. I have a combination of each in my 401(k). This is a good strategy because it spreads the risk so that you are less likely to suffer a dramatic loss if a single company or a particular sector takes a significant loss in the stock market.

Your investment strategy should depend on where you are in your life. Someone close to retirement should pick more conservative investments, whereas a young, single person might decide to invest in funds with more risk. The up side to 401(k)s and 403(b)s is they are tax deferred, meaning that you do not pay taxes on the investment until you start collecting in retirement.

In order to participate in your company's 401(k)/403(b) plan, contact your human resources department or payroll department to find out what investment options you have. The most common way to participate is to have a percentage of your pay removed directly from your paycheck. After awhile, you will not miss the money taken out every month that is invested in your 401(k)/403(b) monthly, but you will notice your net worth increasing steadily.

> Maximize your contribution to get all of the matching funds your employer will contribute to your retirement.

Here is a word of encouragement: Maximize your contribution to get all of the matching funds your employer will contribute to your retirement. For instance, contribute at least the full 6% if your employer will match 50% of your contribution up to 6% of your eligible compensation (which is common). When you add the employer contribution of 3%, you have already gained 50% on your contribution before you start investing. What a great deal! If you make $30,000 per year and invest 6% of this income in your 401(k), under the 50% matching up to 6% rule, your contribution would be $1,800 per year. Your company would contribute $900, so your complete contribution would be $2,700 for the year. It is amazing how many people do not take advantage of this benefit. It is free money. Who wouldn't sign up for free money?

Now here is a word of caution: Limit your investments in single securities, especially your employer's stock. The horror of losing the majority of your retirement like many Enron and Lucent employees could have been avoided if those employees had diversified their

401(k). This works. I know a person who has been retired for three years and is supporting his family completely with his accumulated 401(k). He projects ten more years of 401(k) withdrawals before he will have to tap into his pension and other assets.

IRAs

For those who do not have a 401(k) plan or want to invest more in a long-term retirement investment, there are individual retirement accounts, IRAs. These accounts are generally in the form of mutual funds, but they can take other forms as well. These accounts are also tax-deferred. There is a form of individual retirement account called a Roth IRA, which is available for investments up to a certain amount every year. Roth IRAs offer you the benefit of investing in an IRA, but you will not have to pay any taxes on the investment after you retire.

The investment amount maximums change yearly. From 2005–2007, an individual can contribute up to $4,000 per year into a Roth. This maximum will go up to $5,000 in 2008 and increase by $500 every year thereafter. If your income exceeds a certain threshold, you are not eligible to participate. You should research this with your financial institution. Most Americans do not earn enough income to be disqualified from participating.

Leveraging Investments

Now that we have taken a look at the major investment tools available to you, let's look at the power of investing. The average return on a long-term investment is approximately 10%. In this case, you can expect that an investment of $10,000 will earn you $1,000 the year you invest on average. This is a simple example of how your money can work for you. The more you invest, the more you will make from your investment. Your money is like having an invisible worker earning more money for you.

Using the example of a $10,000 initial investment assuming a 10% annual return, if you do not invest another dime you can expect these results:

Year 1	$11,000.00
Year 2	$12,100.00
Year 3	$13,310.00
Year 4	$14,641.00
Year 5	$16,105.10

After five years, that $10,000 at a 10% rate of return will have earned $6,105.10. That is not bad for doing nothing but making a single investment. Imagine if you systematically invested over time. I cannot stress enough how important it is to invest!

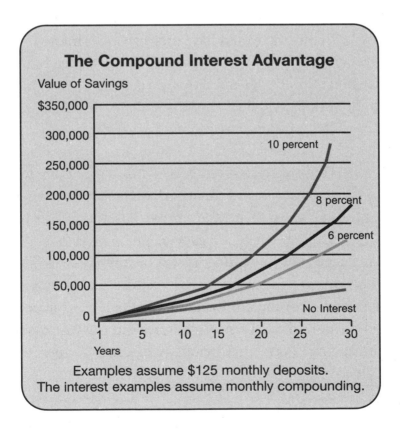

The Compound Interest Advantage

Examples assume $125 monthly deposits.
The interest examples assume monthly compounding.

The preceding chart comes from the website of the Federal Reserve Bank of Dallas,[6] and it graphically shows the value of investing $125 monthly over a period of time. If you started saving at the age of 35 without having saved a dime previously, you would have nearly $300,000 for retirement if that money were to be invested in an average mutual fund with 10% return. Imagine how much you would have saved for retirement had you started at the age of 22!

Let's look at the value of investing over a longer period of time. Let's say that someone aged 25 decides that he wants to be a millionaire in his lifetime, but he has not even started investing. Does this sound impossible? It is definitely possible! How much would this twenty-five year-old have to invest in order to accumulate $1 million? Would he have to invest $1,000 per month? No! If he invests $250 per month in a conservative mutual fund with a 12% return over 32 years, he would have more than $1 million when he reaches the age of 57. Let's say this same person started out with an initial investment of $5,000 and invested $250 per month. He would be worth more than $1 million in 30 years!

That is really a conservative estimate. If this same man had also freed himself of debt and owned a home, his net worth would be even greater. His financial success would be passed on to future generations who, with good financial management, could pass these blessings down to their children. We have the power today to become the starting point of a legacy of prosperity.

This is the power of investing. If we control our spending to the point where we are maximizing our investments, we can realize financial freedom beyond our imagination. Once we gain control of our spending and rid ourselves of debt, we can put that much more into appreciating assets and reach our goals sooner than we ever imagined.

6. Federal Reserve Bank of Dallas, "Building Wealth: Chapter 3, Save and Invest," http://www.dallasfed.org/ca/wealth/pdfs/3.pdf (accessed April 26, 2005).

Rule of 72

Previously, we discussed the power of compounding interest. The Rule of 72 is a shortcut to understanding how your investments can work for you. The Rule of 72 is simply dividing the number 72 by your rate of return to determine how long it will take to double your investment. Let's say that you invest $1,000 in a mutual fund that yields a 12% return. If you divide 72 by 12, you get 6. It will take six years for that $1,000 to become $2,000. By the same token, that $2,000 will be $4,000 in another six years. That compounding continues even if you do not invest anything else into the mutual fund. Compounding exponentially increases your earnings when you invest consistently.

The Fear of Investing

It is natural to fear investing, especially if you do not understand how markets work. Over the long run, the stock market increases in value. There are periods when the stock market takes a big hit like the late 90s when the Dot.com bubble burst or post-9/11. When this happens, your investments will also decrease in value. Dips in the market can happen for several reasons. Investors grow concerned about the economy or world events, and sell their stocks. This decreases the demand for stocks which drives the prices of stock down. That decrease in stock price affects the value of your investments.

> Even if the market dips for a time, by steadily investing over the long haul, you can achieve great results.

You should not fear short-term dips in the market. The stock market has consistently increased in value over its history. If you diversify your investments and stay for the long haul, you can expect your investment portfolio to grow. History is on your side. Since its inception, the New York Stock Exchange has returned an average rate of 11% per year even through the Great Depression and a number of recessions. Decide to invest on a monthly basis. Then, set up an account to automatically deposit a specified amount every month, and do not fear the dips. Dollar cost averaging will help smooth out the dips in the market along the way.

Dollar Cost Averaging

Even if the market dips for a time, by steadily investing over the long haul, you can achieve great results. This is called *dollar cost averaging*. The following table shows how dollar cost averaging works over a 17-month period.

Dollar Cost Averaging Example

Month	Stock Price	Monthly Investment	Number of Stock Shares	Aggregate Number of Stock Shares	Stock Value per Month
1	$ 15.00	$ 300.00	20.00	20.00	$ 300.00
2	14.50	300.00	20.69	40.69	590.00
3	14.00	300.00	21.43	62.12	869.68
4	13.50	300.00	22.22	84.34	1,138.59
5	13.00	300.00	23.08	107.42	1,396.46
6	12.50	300.00	24.00	131.42	1,642.75
7	12.00	300.00	25.00	156.42	1,877.04
8	11.50	300.00	26.09	182.50	2,098.95
9	11.00	300.00	27.27	209.77	2,307.47
10	11.50	300.00	26.09	235.86	2,712.39
11	12.00	300.00	25.00	260.86	3,130.32
12	12.50	300.00	24.00	284.86	3,560.75
13	13.00	300.00	23.08	307.94	4,003.22
14	13.50	300.00	22.22	330.16	4,457.16
15	14.00	300.00	21.43	351.59	4,922.26
16	14.50	300.00	20.69	372.28	5,398.06
17	15.00	300.00	20.00	392.28	**5,884.20**
Total Investment		$ 5,100.00			

The first column lists the month of the investment. The second column represents the price per share of the stock or mutual fund that Steady Eddie is purchasing each month. The third column is the dollar amount he invests. The fourth column is the number of shares of stock he gets for the $300 he is investing. The fifth column is the total number of shares he owns at the point of purchase every month. The final column is the cumulative value of the stock every month.

If you notice, the mutual fund price starts at $15.00. Over seventeen months, the price dips to a low of $11.00 during this economic downturn. After a number of months, the fund's value returns to its original value of $15.00. Although the fund did not gain a penny in value, Steady Eddie has earned a return of $784.22 in a down market because his number of shares has grown.

This is an example of the power of leveraging your resources. A disciplined investment approach will increase your net worth even in a down economy. Because Steady Eddie consistently invested his $5,100 over seventeen months, he earned money even though the value of the mutual fund dipped significantly and only returned to its original value.

Investments are critical to long-range financial success. The few hundred dollars you invest today could be worth millions over time. The combination of long-term growth and dollar cost averaging will profit you richly. Do not fret over your investments every month. Pick a few solid investments with a strong track record over a number of years and keep investing. Periodically, re-evaluate the amount you are investing and the types of investments, but do not get in a situation where you are constantly moving your investment around chasing after what is hot today.

Homeownership

Most people's largest investment is their home. Real estate is an appreciating asset. Homes have a tremendous value to us besides the financial benefit. Homes are where many of our memories reside. It is incredible that we can own something with so much intrinsic and financial value.

However, real estate is like any other investment. There are risks, and it can fluctuate in value. However, on average, homes increase in value a little more than 5% per year. Every month you pay the mortgage, you are lowering the amount owed on the mortgage while the value increases. Additionally, you can realize tax benefits from homeownership, which allows you to keep more of your paycheck.

Home ownership is a better deal than renting. First, you establish a fixed mortgage expense. Unlike rent, your mortgage will not be raised. Secondly, you realize a tax benefit, and thirdly, you own an appreciating asset. Home ownership typically requires a down payment of at least five percent of the value of the home. With good credit, you can get more home for your mortgage payment than you would get for the same amount in rent because you will be rewarded with a lower interest rate.

When you buy a home, you are controlling a larger asset for a relatively small down payment. Let's say you are purchasing a home for $150,000. You will need $15,000, which a includes 5% down payment and 5% for closing costs (attorney fees, real estate agent commission, and first month's mortgage) to purchase the home. You will own a property worth $150,000 for $15,000. You will have to pay the mortgage and taxes. After the taxes and interest on the home loan, the rest of the money will go to paying down the remaining $142,500 balance on the mortgage.

Now, let's assume the $150,000 home you just purchased is appreciating at 5% per year. After one year of owning the home, the house is worth $157,500. You paid $15,000 to control that asset.

At the end of one year, let's say that you have paid $1,500 in principal. If you were to sell the property, the gross cash value of the home to you would be $16,500, which is $1,500 (principal) + $7,500 (down payment) + $7,500 (appreciation). That isn't even counting the tax savings from homeownership!

There are programs that assist former government employees, such as veterans, with buying homes without a down payment. Veterans Administration (VA) loans are a great resource. A VA loan

Homeownership provides you with leverage.

helped me purchase my first home. When I sold my modest home that I bought using my VA loan, I made a nice profit over a short period of time. The profit from my first home was used for the down payment and closing costs on my next home. There was even enough left to help furnish my new home and pay off some debt.

Make use of all the benefits that are afforded to you, especially when it assists you in owning an appreciating asset.

Homeownership provides you with leverage. You can borrow against your home. You can also use the equity in your home to help start that business that you dreamed of starting. Be cautious in doing this. Too often people freely take second and third mortgages, which can put you in a financial bind, especially if the home is not appreciating much. Still, keep in mind that homeownership provides you with financial flexibility that can come in handy.

If you are currently renting and your dream is to own a home, purchasing real estate, even a small property, would be a wise decision. I feel so strongly about homeownership that I made a point of writing a chapter on it. In the chapter on homeownership, I will take you step by step through the home-buying process. Budgeting to own a home is a great financial discipline, and eventually owning an appreciating asset will go further in helping you reach your net worth goal.

Investment Property

The same principles of homeownership are true for investment property. The only difference is that your renters pay your mortgage and provide you with extra income for home repair and vacancy between renters. Just as in homeownership, you are leveraging a relatively small amount of cash to control and profit from a high value investment. Investment properties are excellent investments when done right. They, too, are appreciating assets that will further increase your net worth.

Another advantage to owning rental property is that over time the homes accumulate equity. Home equity is like having a room with an adjustable ceiling filled to the top with water. As you pay the principal, the water level decreases. Over time, as the property increases in value, the ceiling rises. The space between the ceiling and the water is your home equity. The tenant pays rent which covers the loan interest, taxes, insurance, and principal. The principal reduces the loan every month. The tenant's rent is helping reduce the water level in the house while time causes the ceiling to elevate. Before you know it, you have a lot of breathing room. That breathing room gives you more options.

Let's say that you own a rental property worth $100,000, and your principal payments have reduced the loan to $90,000 over four years. Now the $100,000 rental property is worth $130,000. You now have $40,000 of equity in that property. You can use that money to invest in other appreciating assets like more rental homes. Some people have a strategy to get the equity to a certain point in their rental homes and live off the rent and equity. No matter what approach you decide to take, you have another stream of income, a safety net of home equity if you hit hard times, and several resources to increase your financial scorecard.

Car Purchases

The biggest depreciating asset most people own is an automobile. Americans have had a century-long love affair with automobiles. Cars are a status symbol. Cars reflect our personalities. Who doesn't like the smell of a new car? Cars are our favorite toys, but let's look at cars from a financial viewpoint.

Cars are bad investments. Let me repeat that. Cars are bad investments. They are necessities for most families, but they are bad investments nonetheless. Remember, the financial scorecard (Net Worth = Assets – Liabilities). Assets are the value of everything you own, so let's determine the value of your car. Chances are you owe more on your car than it is worth, which hurts your net

Cars are bad investments.

worth. Go to your local bank or pull up a blue book online. A good resource is www.nadaguides.com. Determine the value of your car today based on the blue book value, and compare that to the loan amount you owe on your car. How does your loan value compare to your car value? As soon as you roll a new car off the lot, you owe more than the car is worth.

Car salespeople are trained to appeal to your ego. When you go on a car lot, they will show you how they can make the payments so you can afford the car you want. One successful tactic is to have you finance a car over a long period of time like seventy-two months. Many people find themselves stretched to meet the payments, and in many cases the value of the car is less than the value of the loan until at least five years into the loan.

This is a major problem. You are stuck with that loan for at least five years. That means that if you wanted to sell or trade the car after four years, you will still owe money on the loan. This severely limits your financial flexibility. If you lost your job and needed to reduce your expenses, you could not sell the car and replace it with a less expensive car because you owe more money on the loan than the car is worth. Secondly, your ability to put more money into appreciating assets is limited. You will have that car payment stuck on your budget as a fixed expense. You are locked in!

> Leasing is paying a monthly fee for the privilege of driving a car that you do not own and probably cannot afford.

Another sales tactic is to convince you to lease a car that is too expensive for you to buy. Leasing is paying a monthly fee for the privilege of driving a car that you do not own and probably cannot afford. When you lease, you do not own the car. It is like paying rent. You pay monthly, and you have to keep the car under a certain amount of mileage over the time of the lease. If you exceed the mileage of the contract, you must pay as much as $.15 for each mile over the limit. When the lease is up, you return the car. You own nothing. Consider how this affects your financial scorecard.

Leasing, like anything else, is not a black and white issue. As a good manager of your blessings, you should know all of the implications of financial decisions that you make. Some people lease because it allows them to enjoy a new car every few years without paying the depreciation penalty. In reality, the dealers will make sure that they profit whether you buy or lease. It is important that you have an overall strategy for your personal finances and determine how owning or leasing fits into your equation. Leasing works for some people because they can write off a lease as a business expense. There may be circumstances that make leasing more attractive in your situation. However, I implore you not to lease a car that you cannot afford to buy. That is a good rule of thumb.

There are a couple of strategies that will increase your financial flexibility and provide you with a reliable car. Pre-owned cars hold their value better than new cars. Today, there are many reputable dealers like AutoNation and CarMax that will sell you a certified pre-owned car with a warranty at a good price. The owner who bought the car new has taken the brunt of the depreciation.

The most sensible option is to save and pay for that new or pre-owned car in cash. That gives you the most financial flexibility. Cash gives you more bargaining leverage with the dealer. and as a result, can save you more money. You also save because you are not taking a loan that will cost thousands of dollars over the course of the loan. Even if you can pay a significant portion of the car in cash, you will leave the lot with an asset that has more value than the loan.

Be smart with your car purchase. Do not pay for more than you can afford. When you go through the exercise of budgeting, you will see quickly how buying an expensive car will impact your budget. You will have a high-dollar figure on the car payment line. Also, the more expensive the car, the more you will pay in insurance and maintenance. These are dollars that could be going toward an appreciating asset, which would help you reach your financial goals even faster.

Consider this: As a rule of thumb, mortgage bankers say that $6 per month equates to $1,000 in home value. If you can pay an additional $120 per month into your home, which is an appreciating asset, you can own a home that is $20,000 more in value than your current home. At 5% appreciation, that is at least an additional $1,000 per year you could be adding to your net worth. The other option is to put those dollars into paying off other debt to reduce the liability side of your scorecard.

Education: A Study in Opportunity Cost

Everything, in one way or another, is all about how you view it. Life and money are about perception. I think about the real difference $2,000 can make. Would it really affect anyone besides me, if I spent a couple of extra thousand dollars on a state-of-the-art stereo or added a few extra features to a new car? I would argue that it could affect your child in a significant way, financially and otherwise.

When I was in business school, a friend of mine who hung out with me and a group of other MBA students decided that she wanted to get her MBA. She applied to a top-20 business school, and the school accepted her. She was really excited about going to graduate school. She liked what she was doing at the time, but it was not challenging enough, and the money was just okay.

One night at a party, I asked her how she was going to pay for graduate school. She told me that she would not have to take a school loan or work a single day. She went on to tell me about how her father had put $3,000 into a mutual fund for his newborn daughter in the early 70s. **Her father invested $3,000 and twenty-eight years later, without contributing another dime, it was worth over $70,000.** That money was enough to pay for her top-tier education and living expenses. She would even have enough left to get started after graduate school. I thought that was amazing!

> Life and money are about perception.

I had to quantify this into tangible terms to understand the impact. Let's say that she was making $50,000 at her old job. After graduating from a top business school, she was considerably more marketable. The average starting salary for graduates from that school was about $90,000. With an MBA, she had more upward mobility. She would be in line for promotions, and she would be groomed for executive positions in the future. Therefore, her salary would increase exponentially over time compared to her salary without a graduate degree. If the difference between her career without a graduate degree and with a graduate degree stayed constant over twenty years, she would earn approximately $800,000 more with her graduate degree.

Those extras on the car or the new stereo that you really did not need cost you a lot more than a few thousand dollars. When you look at the lost opportunity cost, that investment in a depreciating asset conservatively cost about one million dollars in future earnings. Also, think about what those few thousand dollars in the early 70s did for my friend. She had the opportunity to focus on school without the distraction of working. She got to broaden her horizons through travel, and some bank lost out on a school loan customer. My point is that the financial decisions you make today make a huge difference in your life and the lives of the people you love. When in doubt, choose to invest in appreciating assets. It can literally change the fortune of your family for generations to come.

Review

1. Invest, invest, invest!

2. Assets are anything you purchase. You can choose to put money into appreciating assets or depreciating assets. The choice is yours.

3. Appreciating assets will exponentially increase your financial scorecard.

4. Take advantage of 401(k)s, 403(b)s and Roth IRAs. Your company and the government are offering you free money. Take it!

5. A little bit of money every month will grow into a mountain of wealth over time.

6. Do not worry about fluctuations in the market. Dollar cost averaging will make up for any short-term losses.

7. Homeownership is awesome! Find a way to own a home whether you are single or married. It is a great investment.

8. Avoid investing in stuff. The money you invest in stuff will work against your long-term vision.

9. There is a huge opportunity cost in spending money on depreciating assets.

Continue the Lesson

Study these Scriptures to understand what God says about investing.

Matthew 25:14–29

I encourage you to go to your Bible, and study this story that Jesus tells about talents, which gives all of the key principles of investing.

1. All that we have to invest is given as a trust from the Lord.
2. Our resources are aligned to our current level of readiness to handle them.
3. Good stewards (managers) study and invest wisely, looking for a good return on investment. The unwise steward is lazy and fearful. He also has a distorted view of the Lord.
4. There is always a time of accountability where the faithful person is rewarded and the unfaithful suffers.

Lesson 6

Avoid Debt at All Cost

"What can be added to the happiness of a man who is in
health, out of debt, and has a clear conscience?"

Adam Smith

One day, I called my dad just to catch up. My parents had been at
their second home in Florida for a month. As we talked, I
commented on how it must be nice to be retired in his early 50s. My
dad revealed to me that it was a struggle to get where he and my
mom are today. The biggest struggle they had was fighting debt.

My dad's tone became serious, and he said, "Son, do whatever
you can to stay out of debt. Debt by itself is bad enough, but when
you consider the effect on your family life, it can be devastating."

"I know debt is bad, but if you can pay at least the minimum
every month then why not live and be happy?"

"That is a very short-sided view. Think about what you would
be able to do if you were debt free. How do you think debt affects
everything you do?"

"It's a burden at times, but I manage it."

"You pay a price every month to carry that debt. If you consider
your finance charges alone, what could you do with that money? If

you had that money freed up, you could tithe and still increase your investments considerably. There is an opportunity cost to debt. Debt keeps you on the earning treadmill longer than you have to be. Debt forces you to work longer hours to pay it off. Debt will keep you distracted from your family and the things you love to do. Stay clear of debt, and you will live an unburdened and prosperous life."

My father is adamant when it comes to debt. He would say to me over and over again to live within my means and stay out of debt. He knew the pain of being saddled with debt. The sleepless nights worrying about making payments and the stress of having to work harder to stay afloat can have a crippling effect on your life.

I really took his words to heart. I thought back to my childhood when both of my parents worked long hours. They would make it to my sporting events when they could, but often work kept them on that treadmill. Then, I thought about my parents today. They are debt free. They travel around the world when they want. They are active in their church and other causes that are important to them, and they have the capacity to be more generous than most. It became clear to me that debt had a huge opportunity cost in money, time spent together as a family, and freedom to pursue interests.

We should be cautious when it comes to debt. Proverbs 22:7 tells us, *"The rich rule over the poor, and the borrower is servant to the lender."* When we borrow, we give creditors reign over us. Living an abundant life means God is the only person who rules over us.

The reality is that most people must have some debt. It is important to learn the different types of debt, and how they affect your financial scorecard.

Types of Debt

There are two types of debt: *constructive debt* and *toxic debt*. I hate toxic debt. Toxic debt keeps me up at night. It should keep you up at night too! Toxic debt is consumer debt that robs you of your wealth. It handcuffs you and keeps you from living the life of freedom you want to live. Toxic debt is like an infestation of termites eating away at your home! This debt is easy to acquire, and it accumulates rapidly. Just like investments in appreciating assets grow exponentially, so does debt, which reduces your financial scorecard. If it isn't kept in check or eliminated altogether, you will be on a financial treadmill of working just to pay the interest.

Toxic debt is acquired from several sources. The world tells us that we need to have the hottest brands. Commercials and television flash images of wealth that we feel the need to imitate despite our limited resources. Our toxic debt problem sometimes stems from watching our parents spend beyond their means. We simply imitate their behavior without realizing the consequences.

> Toxic debt is consumer debt that robs you of your wealth...Constructive debt is debt you use to build your vision.

Let's play our own game from this point forward. Let's see television and those illusions of grandeur for what they are—sales pitches that drag us into stores spending money on items of little value. We'll examine how this toxic debt can get us in deep financial trouble and cripple our ability to advance financially.

Constructive debt is better, but even it should be kept to a minimum. Constructive debt is debt that you use to build your vision. It allows you the resources to buy a home or start a business. An example of constructive debt is your home mortgage. This is debt that you use to leverage your existing wealth to create more wealth. Your home generally increases in value over time, so as that home loan is being retired, you are gaining the upside of the appreciation of your property while reducing the debt. The difference in the value of the home and the mortgage is equity. Equity is money that is yours. It is considered an asset in your net worth equation.

Other types of constructive debt are small business loans and student loans. These forms of debt assist you in acquiring means of producing wealth. Your education will allow you to earn more. The small business loan will allow you to make your business successful.

> Constructive debt is a gamble that the money will allow you to earn considerably more than the cost of the debt.

Yet, be wary of constructive debt. Often, this type of debt is abused. Students will often take loans far in excess of what they need without considering the monthly payments they will have to make for several years to pay it off. Some people start businesses and spend freely as if the money was free, but even constructive debt has a cost. Constructive debt is a gamble. You are gambling that the money from the debt will allow you to earn considerably more than the cost of the debt. Minimize your constructive debt and maximize the benefit that the constructive debt brings you.

Rule of 72 Revisited

We discussed the Rule of 72 in the chapter on investing. Just as the Rule of 72 tells you how long it will take to double an investment, it works the same way with debt. Assume you borrow $10,000 from your bank at an interest rate of 12%. If you divide 72 by 12, you get 6. After carrying that debt for six years, you will have paid your bank $20,000 for the $10,000 you borrowed. Imagine if you did not have that debt. You could put the money you paid the bank into investments to increase your financial scorecard.

Compounding interest is a sword that cuts both ways. Make sure that you are on the right side of the Rule of 72. Kill your toxic debt so you can significantly increase your financial scorecard by taking money that would be compounding for your bank or credit card and have it work for you in appreciating assets.

Toxic Debt

Now, let's work on efficiently killing your toxic debt so you can get that money working for you on the right side of your financial scorecard equation. Let's take a look at a toxic debt portfolio by pretending you have the following debt:

Debt Accounts

Card Name	Current Balance	APR	Finance Charges	Payment	New Balance
Macy's	$ 3,000.00	22%	$ 55.00	$ 60.00	$ 2,995.00
Discover	7,000.00	17%	113.23	120.00	6,993.23
Visa	11,000.00	15%	154.20	160.00	10,994.20
Totals	$ 21,000.00		322.43	$ 340.00	$ 20,982.43

NOTE: APR is Annual Percentage Rate. This is the rate of interest you are charged on the balance.

As you can see, the privilege of having the clothes, car and other depreciating assets you purchased is costing you $322.43 per month. Remember the person we discussed before in the appreciating assets section became a millionaire investing $250 per month. Your finance charges alone are costing you dearly. To put this in perspective, the cost of your toxic debt could buy a new top brand color television every month. If you invested the $340 you are paying to reduce your debt at 12% return per year in a mutual fund, you would have a million dollars in twenty-four years. This example shows an opportunity cost in real dollars. Toxic debt is expensive!

The Debt Ladder

In the preceding example, you are paying random amounts to pay off your debt. It will take you several years to pay off this debt at this rate. It is like jogging up an escalator. For all the energy you expend, you are not making much progress. Your net worth on your financial scorecard will stay low. We want to employ strategies that will help you get up the escalator faster and improve the health of your financial scorecard.

The optimal strategy to get up that escalator faster is to pay off the most expensive debt first, meaning the debt with the highest annual percentage rate (APR). The debt ladder is a method of efficiently decreasing your debt by prioritizing each bill from the highest to the lowest interest rate. You pay off the debt that costs you the most while continuing to pay the minimum on all your other accounts.

To demonstrate the debt ladder, let's assume you pay the bare minimum, your finance charges, on all your debt except the one with the highest interest rate. However, you have budgeted well and can put $600 per month toward your debt. The following tables provide a snapshot of the first and twelfth months of using the debt ladder vs. making equal payments. Look at your payments. Note that your minimum payments will be more than just the finance charges in most cases. This example of the debt ladder shows the power of paying your high interest debt first. Do you see the difference in debt reduction between the equal payment method and the strategy of paying off the bill with the highest interest rate first?

Debt Ladder Method

Month 1

Card Name	Current Balance	APR	Finance Charges	Payment	New Balance
Macy's	$ 3,000.00	22%	$ 55.00	$ 332.57	$ 2,722.43
Discover	7,000.00	17%	113.23	113.23	7,000.00
Visa	11,000.00	15%	154.20	154.20	11,000.00
Totals	$ 21,000.00		$ 322.43	$ 600.00	$ 20,722.43

Month 12

Card Name	Current Balance	APR	Finance Charges	Payment	New Balance
Macy's	$ (0.00)	22%	$ (0.00)	$ (0.00)	$ (0.00)
Discover	5,414.80	17%	87.58	445.80	4,953.77
Visa	11,000.00	15%	154.20	154.20	11,000.00
Totals	16,414.80		$ 241.78	$ 600.00	$ 15,953.77

Paying the higher interest rate first really makes a big difference. Using the above example, you can see the power of paying your high interest debt first, no matter what the balances are. The Macy's card now has a zero balance, and you can now focus your energy on the next highest interest debt, the Discover card.

Equal Payment Method

Month 1

Card Name	Current Balance	APR	Finance Charges	Payment	New Balance
Macy's	$ 3,000.00	22%	$ 55.00	$ 200.00	$ 2,855.00
Discover	7,000.00	17%	113.23	200.00	6,913.23
Visa	11,000.00	15%	154.20	200.00	10,954.20
Totals	$ 21,000.00		$ 322.43	$ 600.00	$20,722.43

Month 12

Card Name	Current Balance	APR	Finance Charges	Payment	New Balance
Macy's	$ 1,250.40	22%	22.92	$ 200.00	$ 1,073.32
Discover	6,135.15	17%	112.47	200.00	6,047.62
Visa	11,019.89	15%	202.01	200.00	11,021.90
Totals	18,405.44		$ 337.40	$ 600.00	$18,142.84

The equal payment method left you with a balance of $18,142.84, but the method of paying the debt with highest interest rate first left you owing $15,953.79. After one year, the debt ladder method increased your net worth to $2,189.05, although you were paying a total of $800 per month in both methods. Also, note how your total finance charges were reduced considerably as you paid your higher interest debt. You saved money every month by squashing your highest interest rate debt first.

Focus on your high interest debt. As you pay off these debts, reward yourself by cutting that credit card up and focusing on the next highest interest debt. This is how you get to zero debt quickly.

The debt ladder is another example of why it is important to have a plan. Let's put together a strategy to reduce your debt and increase your wealth. Get out some paper and follow these steps:

1. List all of your toxic debt.
2. Record the current balance, APR, and amount of the finance charge on your last statement and your current payment for each bill.
3. Add a column for new payment.

Now that you have a clear picture of your debt portfolio, you can execute the following plan to get rid of your toxic debt:

1. Prioritize your debt using the debt ladder. Pay off the highest interest debt first.
2. Stop using credit cards!
3. Search for better rates.
4. Consider consolidating your debt into one low-interest loan.

Prioritize Payments

Many people just pay off their debts haphazardly. That practice is counterproductive. In the debt ladder example, we demonstrated the power of prioritizing high interest debt. Earlier in this chapter, we showed you the interest rate or finance charge. Paying the finance charges does not reduce your debt at all. This just keeps the balance the same. Focus on reducing the highest interest debt first. This will reduce your debt faster than spreading the payments across your debt evenly. Hence, you will get out of debt faster.

Once you realize how much debt costs on a monthly basis, you will be motivated to get rid of it. At some point, I looked at my finance charges and was blown away. I was paying more in finance charges than I was paying on my car payment! I could have been well on my way to becoming a millionaire if I had invested that money. I quickly realized that the longer I remained tied to those finance charges, the longer I would be a prisoner of toxic debt.

Stop Using Credit Cards

Commit to staying within your budget. You might consider reducing your entertainment expenses. Resist making unnecessary purchases. When you can, find deals to save money. Whatever you do, stop using credit cards! One excellent technique is to freeze the cards. Fill a zip lock bag with water, insert the cards, and then, throw the bag in the freezer. When you have the urge to make an impulsive purchase, you will have to thaw out the cards. By the time the cards thaw, you will have thought twice about making that purchase.

Another tactic to reduce spending and stay within your budget is to write down all of your expenses as you spend. This will make you aware of all of your purchases. The physical action of writing down expenses, as discussed previously, makes you conscious of your spending. Then, at the end of every month, evaluate where you spent your money and how you spent it.

My big pet peeve is department store cards. They are higher in interest than any of the major credit cards. Department stores will lure you into getting a card by offering you ten percent off of purchases when you get the card. They make the offer betting that you take the bait. Accepting these promotions will increase the likelihood of your sliding into a financial abyss.

They also offer 0% interest for 90 days. This is another bet. They are betting that you will continue to spend on their card and become further indebted to them. Once the 90 days are up, the interest will kick in if the account is not paid in full at that time. These companies have done their homework. They know the characteristics and habits of people who get their cards. They are laying in wait. Don't fall prey to their indebtedness tactics.

Search for a Better Rate

Credit card companies will charge you as much as they can. It is your responsibility to call them about the rates they are charging you. If your credit is sound, they know that you have other options. More times than not, you can negotiate a better rate than what they are charging you. If you do not ask, you will not receive. They want to keep you as a customer. Make them accomplices in your escape from debt.

Let's assume you made those calls to your credit card companies and got them to lower the rates on all of your cards. Let's examine your debt before and after lowering your rates. The first table shows your payments before you called the credit card companies. The second table shows what you would be paying after negotiating lower interest rates on your credit cards.

Before Asking for a Lower Rate

Card Name	Current Balance	APR	Finance Charges	Payment	New Balance
Macy's	$ 3,000.00	22%	$ 55.00	$ 332.57	$ 2,722.43
Discover	$ 7,000.00	17%	113.23	$ 113.23	7,000.00
Visa	$ 11,000.00	15%	154.20	$ 154.20	11,000.00
Totals	$21,000.00		$ 322.43	$600.00	$ 20,722.43

After Asking for a Lower Rate

Card Name	Current Balance	APR	Finance Charges	Payment	New Balance
Macy's	$ 3,000.00	17%	$ 48.53	$ 378.51	$ 2,670.02
Discover	7,000.00	15%	98.13	98.13	7,000.00
Visa	11,000.00	12%	123.36	123.36	11,000.00
Totals	$ 21,000.00		$ 270.02	$ 600.00	$ 20,670.02

Your monthly interest before you asked for reduced rates was $322.43. With the slightly reduced rates, you are now paying $270.02 in finance charges. This is a savings of $52.41 per month. Using the debt ladder and asking for lower rates will get the liabilities side of your financial scorecard lower in a hurry. That $52.41 that you save can be used to pay a phone bill, invest in an appreciating asset, or pay your debt off faster; whereas before, it was doing nothing for you.

Although $52.41 is a small dent, that small dent will make a tremendous difference over time. Think about it. This savings is just for picking up the phone and making a few phone calls. You just earned an extra $52.41 in that month from thirty minutes on the phone with your creditors asking for a lower rate. Remember, you have leverage. You have the option of canceling the card, which might be a good idea anyway. In the past, I have threatened to cancel a card if I did not get a substantially lower rate, and the creditor obliged. Try it. These companies will not give you anything that you do not ask for.

Also, you should perform plastic surgery. Destroy all of your cards except one. Cut the others up and freeze the one low-interest card that you save. In fact, you do not have to wait until the credit card is paid off to cancel it. Get on the phone and cancel those cards. In the credit section, we will discuss another benefit of doing this besides the obvious.

Debt Consolidation

I proceed with caution telling you about debt consolidation. There are a lot of unscrupulous, predatory lenders who will lead you to believe you are getting a great deal only to pull a bait and switch. Stay away from these lenders. They have worked for years refining their deception.

Also, make sure you read and understand the fine print before you move your debt over to another credit card. Some credit card companies offer you 0% interest for a few months as a reward for transferring your debt to their card. However, be aware that many of these credit card companies will charge you 3% on the amount being transferred, and they can potentially hit you with an interest rate that is as high as the other card after the promotion period.

Another potential catch is high late fees as a condition of transferring the debt from another card. So, if you are transferring $10,000 to a credit card with this great offer, do not be surprised when the first bill arrives and the balance is $10,300. Also, if you are even a day late paying, they could slap you with a late fee of $50 or more. The 3% transfer fee and other conditions around transferring that debt may be worth it, but do the math and be aware of the transfer charges and other potential costs before you do it.

Debt consolidation is a good idea in theory, but it requires real discipline to pull it off. First, go to a reputable bank to get an estimate on different finance products they have available. These products may vary depending on the bank, but if it is a major bank, you can trust that they are operating under strict legal rules. If you do go the debt consolidation route, destroy the cards that you consolidated. Otherwise, you will run the risk of digging yourself into a bigger hole by running up the credit cards again.

Debt consolidation serves a couple of purposes. It can set your debt payments on a predictable fixed schedule, which will make it easier to budget. Secondly, debt consolidation from a reputable bank is generally offered at a lower interest rate than most credit cards. This will help take some of the sting out of those finance charges that will keep you on the debt treadmill. Let debt consolidation be a tool for you in your master plan for prosperity, but be wise in using it.

Now that you have a budget and a strategy for reducing debt, you can go on the offensive. Offense in the financial world is investments from savings. When your debt is gone, all of those dollars that would have gone to pay finance charges and principal on your debt can be put to work multiplying your "talent." Debt is designed to keep you paying finance charges because that is how creditors make their money. Let them make their living at someone else's expense, not yours.

Review

1. Stay clear of debt!

2. There are two types of debt—toxic and constructive. Avoid toxic debt altogether, and minimize the use of constructive debt.

3. Debt is expensive in so many different ways. Focus on freeing yourself of this burden.

4. Create a game plan, and set a schedule for reducing your debt. Utilize the debt ladder.

5. Practice plastic surgery. Cut up those cards.

6. Search for a better interest rate. A few minutes on the phone can make a real impact on your payments.

7. Consolidate debt, but be careful about which company you choose to use. Destroy the credit cards you consolidate.

8. There is an opportunity cost associated with debt. If you are continually paying on debt, you miss the opportunity to invest in your future.

Continuing the Lesson

Study these Scriptures to learn more on God's principles for handling debt.

Psalm 37:21

The wicked borrow and do not repay, but the righteous give generously.

Deuteronomy 28:12–14

[12]The LORD will open the heavens, the storehouse of his bounty, to send rain on your land in season and to bless all the work of your hands. You will lend to many nations but will borrow from none. [13]The LORD will make you the head, not the tail. If you pay attention to the commands of the LORD your God that I give you this day and carefully follow them, you will always be at the top, never at the bottom. [14]Do not turn aside from any of the commands I give you today, to the right or to the left, following other gods and serving them.

Lesson 7

Stay Trustworthy, Keep Good Credit

"Remember that credit is money."

Benjamin Franklin

I had been going through a difficult time with a tenant who had not paid his rent for two months. I was in the process of evicting him. My dad and I were playing a round of golf, and I asked him, "How can people just decide to not pay their bills?" It was completely beyond me how someone could do that. We started talking about credit and how it related to trustworthiness.

My dad listened to me complain for awhile and said, "Son, there is nothing more important than being trusted. When it comes to credit, not being trusted is expensive."

"Why wouldn't someone just be trustworthy and pay their debts?"

"Excessive debt can put you in a position where you cannot make payments. When you do not make payments, companies are keeping tabs on your trustworthiness. I don't think most people intend to refuse to pay their creditors. Most people dig themselves into a hole so deep by living beyond their means, which leads to spending money they don't have. When they become unemployed or they just borrow so much that they can't pay, they miss payments or refuse payment altogether."

"I hear about people all the time who file bankruptcy. They seem to survive it."

"Those people survive it, but it comes at an expense. They will be marked as not being credit worthy. They will pay more for the money they borrow. Besides, can you imagine Jesus filing for bankruptcy? You pay what you owe, and you will be blessed for it."

My father always taught me that credit is a measure of your integrity. It is both biblical and honorable to live up to your commitments. If you are deemed to be a credit risk, companies are simply saying that you cannot be trusted. Your bad credit score is a red flag that tells anyone who is considering you for a loan that you cannot be trusted.

Think about this in personal terms. Can you imagine a friend or family member telling a person who is considering loaning you money that he should not do it because there is a good chance you will not pay it back? That would be insulting! Millions of Americans, today, have poor credit. They are deemed untrustworthy, and they pay a price for that.

Credit is critical to being able to accomplish your financial goals. Without credit, you are fighting an uphill battle. With bad credit, you are severely hamstrung. Even with constructive debt, you will have to pay more for that money than someone with good credit. In this chapter, we will discuss the implications of good credit and explain how credit works. Additionally, we will discuss strategies to improve your credit rating.

The Value of Good Credit

Credit is simply a measure of how well you repay money. The more credit worthy a person is, the less creditors charge them for their debt. When companies loan money to borrowers, they are taking a risk. They have to make at least the rate of inflation or they will lose money. That is the first risk. Then, they have to determine whether you can pay off the debt. If your credit is good, they consider you a lower risk borrower, so they offer you attractive rates to entice you to borrow. If your credit is bad, you present a higher risk, so they offer you a higher rate to insure that, even if you default, they will make enough that they will not lose money.

This concept is no different from the scenario discussed earlier with bonds. If you are a risk to pay back the money, you have to pay more for the privilege of borrowing. If you are credit worthy, then the company knows, based on your

> Credit is simply a measure of how well you repay money.

history, that you will pay back the loan, so they charge you less. The credit worthy individual is a hot commodity. Companies will beg you to borrow money because your credit score tells them that you will not default on the loan.

Your credit report is checked whenever you go to rent an apartment or borrow money for a car or home. Your credit report shows your history of borrowing and paying off debt. Late payments, particularly payments past 90 days, hurt your credit rating. Credit history is a strong predictor of a borrower's behavior. If your credit history is bad, chances are you may have more late payments, which makes you a borrowing risk.

That bad credit history will cost you. Credit card companies and banks build in extra interest for people with a bad credit history. In some cases, they will deem you too much of a risk to lend you money. As demonstrated earlier with the debt ladder example, you can see that higher interest will cost you significantly more than low interest. Over the course of a mortgage, you could end up paying more than twice as much in interest than a person with a strong credit history.

A strong credit history will give you the flexibility to employ some of the tactics discussed in the debt section. With a poor credit history, you are lucky to be able to borrow any money; let alone demand a lower interest rate. Do not take your credit history lightly. Poor credit will hinder you from reaching your financial goals.

Credit is money. On a home loan, if your credit is shaky, you will have to accept a higher interest loan than a person with solid credit. This could amount to hundreds of dollars a month more in interest charges. Those hundreds of dollars represent more money you could be investing in your financial freedom.

Understanding Your Credit Report

Many people do not even know their credit history. You are entitled to know. Your lenders surely know, so you should know at least what they do. You should check your credit once a year. Equifax, Experian, and TransUnion are major credit bureaus that track your credit history. You can call Equifax at (800) 685-1111 or visit their website at www.equifax.com to request your free credit report once a year.

These credit bureaus use different tools to determine your credit worthiness. The most common is FICO, which stands for Fair Isaac and Company. The components of your FICO score are payment history, amounts owed, length of credit history, new credit, and types of credit used. The general percentage of importance is shown in the following chart.[7]

---

7. myFICO, "What's In Your Score," www.myfico.com/CreditEducation/WhatsInYourScore.aspx (accessed April 27, 2005).

Credit Score Components

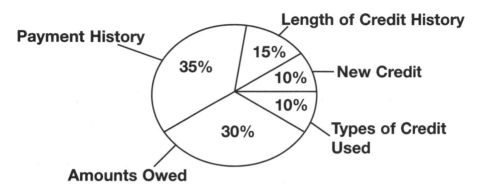

Payment history takes into account several different criteria. The criteria examined are account payment information, presence of adverse public records (bankruptcy, past due items, liens), severity of delinquency, amount past due on delinquent accounts, time since past due items, number of past due items, and number of accounts paid on time. Payment history takes into account that you have been a model borrower for the last five years even if you were delinquent on a payment five years ago.

Amounts owed include:
- Total amount owed on all accounts
- Amounts owed on specific types of accounts
- Lack of a specific type of balance
- Number of accounts with balances
- Proportion of credit lines used
- Proportion of installment loan amounts still owed[8]

The credit bureau wants to be sure that you do not have too much rope to hang yourself. If you have several accounts open, they realize that you can borrow from those open accounts and potentially stretch yourself so thin that you cannot pay on the loan for which you are applying. Also, if you have several balances

8. Ibid.

outstanding, they know that you are still on the hook for money from several other companies. This makes you a greater risk, which affects your score.

Previously, I mentioned closing accounts that are still open. The reason this makes sense is that it lowers the number of credit lines used, which helps your score. Do not do this as a short-term solution to raise your score. Do this to remove the temptation of using those accounts. This is the credit equivalent of burning your bridges. You will be making a commitment to go forward, being responsible with your use of credit.

Some people who pay on time consistently have trouble borrowing money. I ran into this issue once. I had no idea why a credit card company declined my application, especially since my credit was good. I discovered that the lender considered me too much of a risk because I had too many open accounts. The accounts had been paid in full, but I never closed them. Some of them were several years old. When you have open accounts, you have more rope to hang yourself.

Let's say that you have four open accounts with a credit line of $5,000 each. You have paid the balance in full and thrown away the card. Technically, if you have not closed the accounts, you can still borrow $20,000. The lender feels you are a risk to borrow more since you could conceivably borrow $20,000 and be in over your head. When you pay off your credit cards or even before you pay off the accounts, close the accounts. This will ultimately enhance your ability to borrow.

Length of credit history is self-explanatory. If you have been borrowing money for a number of years and have paid them on time, you have established a track record of dependability that will boost your score. The longer you show a good track record, the better your score.

New credit considers the number of recently opened accounts, number of recent credit inquiries, amount of time since recent account openings, time since credit inquiries, and re-establishment of positive credit history following past payment problems. Once again, the lender wants to make sure that you have not over extended yourself. Having several new lines of credit adversely affects your score.

Do not be alarmed. No single issue mentioned above will sink your credit. The score considers several factors. If you have a reasonable amount of open accounts and you do not have any recent delinquencies, you should be in decent shape. However, you should strive to make your credit score as high as possible because it will allow you to get credit at a lower interest rate. For additional information, go to www.myfico.com.

Your credit report shows a lot of information about your credit history. You will find dates, credits, available balances, open accounts, lenders, and payment history. Sometimes there are errors in the report. You can correct those errors by contacting the lender and reporting the error to the credit bureau. Keep all of your credit card statements, particularly the ones that are paid in full. The credit bureau will want to see evidence of the error.

> You should strive to make your credit score as high as possible because it will allow you to get credit at a lower interest rate.

Even if you are not turned down for a credit card or loan, you will be offered a higher interest rate on any money you borrow, if you neglect to clean up your credit history. Credit reports are valuable tools to understanding what lenders see in you. When you are buying that dream house, you want to have the lowest payments possible for the type of loan you are getting. Before making any major purchase, get a credit report and make sure there is nothing that prevents you from getting the lowest rate possible.

If you run into a problem making a payment on time, be proactive. Contact the lender and work out an arrangement to make some sort of payment. Most lenders are eager to work with borrowers who make an effort. In return, they will refrain from filing negative credit history information. The lender wants to receive their money, so they will usually work with you to pay off your debt.

Now that we have gone through all the different components that can affect your score, you are probably wondering what is considered a good score and a bad score. The answer is: It depends on the lender. Here is an example from www.fico.com that might help you understand the difference your FICO score can make.[9]

Impact of FICO Score

FICO Score	Interest Rate	Monthly Payment
720-850	5.81%	$ 881.00
700-719	5.94%	893.00
675-699	6.47%	946.00
620-674	7.62%	1,062.00
560-619	8.53%	1,157.00
500-559	9.29%	$ 1,238.00

NOTE: The above numbers are an example only. The actual rates will vary depending on the lender.

If you have already created a bad credit history, there are ways to fix the problem over time. Contact the lender you have not paid, and make arrangements to settle your debt. Also, keep making timely payments. Two years of consistent, on-time payments will put you in better standing. If you are in serious debt and need help, there are non-profit organizations like Consumer Credit Counseling that will act as a go-between and work with you and your lenders to straighten out your credit. They will also further educate you on credit history and debt management.

Bankruptcy should be considered a last resort. Too many people get in over their heads, and instead of taking on the difficult

9. myFICO, "Save the Smart Way," www.myfico.com (accessed April 27, 2005).

task of paying off the debt, they file bankruptcy. That is not just seven years of bad luck. It is seven years of bad credit. If you are in a financial bind, there are a number of ways to work through it. It will require hard work and sacrifice, but it is much better than having that black mark on your credit or being disobedient to God. Bankruptcy is the ultimate symbol of poor stewardship and untrustworthiness.

Bad Credit Story

I own rental homes, so I deal with people who are seeking homes for their families. The first thing I do is check their credit. If their credit is bad, I will either turn them away or charge them more and take a larger deposit to cover my risk. That person will have to pay considerably more for the privilege of renting a home from me.

> Bankruptcy should be considered a last resort.

Oftentimes, they are renting because their credit prevents them from qualifying for a home loan. One of my rental homes is a $165,000 house. Because of my good credit, I got the lowest loan available for a 30-year mortgage. My payments are $950 per month. The renter with bad credit has to pay me $1,250 per month to rent the home. Additionally, that person had to pay me two months rent as a deposit instead of the traditional one month. That person is out of pocket for thousands of dollars just to rent, not own. Additionally he's paying $300 more a month than I am paying with excellent credit.

If someone were to extend a loan this person with bad credit, he would pay at least 4% more than I pay. Additionally, the lender would ask for more money down. That $165,000 house would cost the person with poor credit tens of thousands more than I would pay over a 30-year period.

Also, consider other loans. The rate for his car loan is higher too. When you figure it all out, he is paying at least $400 more than I would pay for the same things. Now, think back to the debt ladder. How much faster could his debt be eliminated with $400 more a month? That $400 dollars invested every month at a 12% rate of return would be worth $1,000,000 in 28 years. If he owned that same home over that period of time, his home would be paid for and his net worth would increase to $1,173,852, assuming the property increased in value at a rate of 7% year over year. Over 30 years, the person with bad credit will leave over $2.1 million dollars on the table. Bad credit is expensive!

Good Credit Story

I know an individual with great credit who wanted to get into real estate. This guy made an average salary, and his credit was excellent. When he found his first rental property, he paid a low interest rate and rented out the home for a little more than his mortgage. After a period of time, he found another rental property. He leveraged his good credit to pay for the house with a little money down. This trend continued. He now owns fifteen properties. His financial scorecard looks great. He has enough equity in his homes to buy even more properties. His properties are going up in value. He is making money from the rent payments. His credit worthiness, even with an average salary, has made him financially well off.

Additionally, he pays less for his car loan, if he even has one. He pays less in mortgage interest on his rental homes, which means that he can be competitive in the rental home market, and he still has a positive cash flow. All of this success did not come from winning the lottery or a ridiculously large salary. It all started with excellent credit. Credit is truly money!

Compare the story of the person with bad credit with the person with excellent credit. Good credit makes a difference in your financial scorecard. The bottom line is that being credit worthy is morally right and financially smart.

Your credit is a reflection of you. If your credit is bad, it tells lenders that you are undisciplined in your spending, and you are not reliable. A strong credit history tells lenders that you are disciplined and responsible. The punishment for being undisciplined and unreliable is high interest. The reward for discipline and responsibility is low interest and access to money whenever you need it. With a good credit history, lenders can help you bolster your financial scorecard by offering you low interest money to buy appreciating assets like homes or cash for businesses. Work on creating a strong credit history. Your options are limitless with a strong credit rating.

Review

1. Credit worthiness is a moral obligation.

2. Being credit worthy will help you reach your financial goals faster.

3. Having bad credit will hurt you financially. Good credit will substantially improve your financial scorecard.

4. Know your credit score, and take decisive action to improve it.

5. Work with your lenders if you are having difficulty making payments. A little communication can save you from being labeled a credit risk.

6. Bankruptcy should be an absolute last resort!

7. Having access to cash enables you to leverage other people's money to acquire appreciating assets and increase your financial scorecard.

Continuing the Lesson

Study these Scriptures to better understand God's view of these topics:

Trustworthiness

Proverbs 3:1–6

[1]My son, do not forget my teaching, but keep my commands in your heart, [2]for they will prolong your life many years and bring you prosperity. [3]Let love and faithfulness never leave you; bind them around your neck, write them on the tablet of your heart. [4]Then you will win favor and a good name in the sight of God and man. [5]Trust in the LORD with all your heart and lean not on your own understanding; [6]in all your ways acknowledge him, and he will make your paths straight.

Bankruptcy

Psalm 37:21

The wicked borrow and do not repay, but the righteous give generously.

Lesson 8

Develop Multiple Streams of Income

"It takes as much imagination to create debt as to create income."

Leonard Orr

One evening years ago, my father and I were talking after dinner. I asked, "Dad, how do most people become wealthy?"

"Son, wealth is like flowing water," he said, "It flows from one person or business to another. Think about a river. It receives water from different sources, and that water flows to other sources. It is fluid."

"But how do you gain wealth if your money is constantly flowing away from you? How can you ever accumulate anything?"

"You are absolutely correct. If you have one stream of income, the income will eventually flow out. However, if you have multiple streams of income, you can pool your resources into a reservoir. Some income will still flow out, but the idea is to have more that stays in the reservoir."

"So, you are saying that if you only have one stream, you are less able to pool resources than if you have multiple streams flowing into your reservoir."

"Exactly. The more streams of income you have, the more resources you will have. The more resources you are able to pool, the more you will be able to accomplish."

That great metaphor has stuck with me to this day. I took some time to consider this concept. I read books on successful people, and the one common thread I saw in financially successful people was that they all received income from different sources. This couldn't have been a coincidence.

Common Streams of Income

In the chapter on assets, we discussed investing in mutual funds, 401(k)s, bonds, and homes. These are common sources of alternative streams of income. These forms of income are the easiest to create. Find one or more of these investment vehicles that fits your risk profile, and invest consistently. These appreciating assets will produce real income.

> The one common thread I saw in financially successful people was that they all received income from different sources.

Let's say that you have $50,000 invested in a mutual fund that averages 10% return per year, and you make a $40,000 per year salary. Your salary in real terms is $45,000. You did no work to produce that extra $5,000. In fact, you created a 12.5% raise for yourself just by investing your money. The beauty of these appreciating assets is that they continue to give you a bigger and bigger raise every year. The next year that investment is $55,000. At the same rate of growth, you can add $5,500 to your salary next year. It is the gift that keeps giving and growing.

Also consider the free money that is out there. If your employer offers a 401(k) plan, they will match 50% of your investment up to 6% of your salary. At $40,000 per year, your 6% 401(k) contribution is $2,400, which means your employer will match that $2,400 with $1,200. That is an additional $1,200 of income. You increased your salary by $1,200, just for investing. It gets even better. That $2,400 that you invested does not count against you as income, so the government taxes you on $37,600 instead of $40,000. At a 25% tax bracket, that equates to $600 in tax savings.

Homes are even better at providing you another stream of income. Let's say you invest in a home worth $110,000. You invest $10,000 as a down payment. To simplify the math, let's assume the home increases 10% per year. At the end of the first year, your home is worth $121,000. That $10,000 down payment has increased your financial scorecard by $11,000. That doesn't include the tax break you will receive for being a homeowner. Take the $5,000 from the mutual fund, the $1,200 from matching 401(k) funds, the $600 in tax savings for the 401(k) contribution, and the $11,000 from the increase in home value (not to mention the tax break). Now, your $40,000 of income has increased to $57,800.

Some might argue that you are paying interest on the mortgage, but that interest is tax deductible and can further increase your tax savings. In many cases, even with interest, you are paying less to buy a home than you would be paying if you rented. If you rented the home, you would be paying money that is only making money for the homeowner, and you get no tax break. You might as well set that money on fire every month.

The common investments like mutual funds and 401(k)s are excellent tools to increase your income immediately. By investing in homes, 401(k)s, and mutual funds, you can create three new streams of income above and beyond your salary.

Hobbies and Income

I am a firm believer that we have more time on our hands than we think. Consider the time you spend sitting in front of the television. Many Americans spend 4–5 hours a day watching television. What if you were to use that time doing something that you love and turning it into a revenue opportunity?

A friend of mine was really into cosmetics. She invested hundreds of dollars into cosmetics every year. She was a salesperson by trade, and she liked socializing with people. A friend of hers introduced her to selling Mary Kay cosmetics. I know that multi-level marketing is not for everyone, but this one fit her. She had the opportunity to share her love for cosmetics, socialize with new people, and make money doing what she enjoyed doing anyway. It only took up a few hours of her time every week, and she looked forward to doing it. She made a few extra hundred dollars per month doing it, and she eventually grew it into a small business that increased steadily over time.

The money that she made doing what she loved doing anyway created another stream of income. She could have invested the earnings. She could have used the earnings to pay down her debt. No matter what she decided to do with the extra income, it was increasing her financial scorecard. Imagine improving your financial situation doing what you love to do.

A guy who used to work with me was a sports fanatic. He had an encyclopedic knowledge of baseball and football statistics. This guy also loved to collect baseball and football cards. He never thought of his passion as a source of income, but it soon became one. He started to realize that the cards and memorabilia that he collected over the years were worth a lot of money. So he spent his weekends doing what he loved to do. He watched sports and attended card shows looking for bargains.

Eventually, he took an early retirement from the company. He was not sure how he would supplement his early retirement money. Then he discovered that baseball and football card manufacturers hired salespeople to attend these conventions and card shows. He found a fulfilling second career attending the same shows that he did before for fun.

We all have hobbies. If you can create another stream of income from that hobby, consider it. It will add to your financial scorecard and potentially set you up for what you really want to do for a living. If you are going to engage in a hobby, why not make money from it?

Second Jobs

A second job does not have to be a bad thing. Typically, when people mention second jobs, all kinds of presumptions pop into our minds. We think they must be struggling to make ends meet. However, second jobs are not taboo as long as they do not adversely affect our primary source of income, and we enjoy doing it.

One of my classmates in grad school had a second job. Her day job was an accountant, and she knew a lot of people in the area. She had a background in accounting, and she loved real estate. So she got her real estate license and sold houses in her free time. When she was too busy to actively sell, she made referrals to other agents through her extensive network. Now, she has a job as a senior manager in the accounting department of a large company, and in her free time makes money doing something she truly enjoys, exploring real estate.

> If you are going to engage in a hobby, why not make money from it?

I went back to my ten-year college reunion. Several of my classmates were college professors at my alma mater. That got me to thinking. I enjoy teaching and speaking, and I have an educational background that qualifies me to teach college. So, I started thinking about ways to turn those passions into another stream of income. I researched all of the local junior colleges and adult education institutions in my area. I sent letters requesting information, and I conducted informational interviews with people who were teaching part-time. I found the perfect fit for me and my schedule, the

University of Phoenix. Classes are in the evening one night a week. My fellow faculty members are also full-time professionals. We have the option of teaching when we want to teach. I found another stream of income, an opportunity to do something I love, and a way to build my resume—all at the same time.

I know of people at all levels of corporate life who have second jobs. Some call them their play jobs. I know people who work at coffee shops on weekends because they like the social interaction. I know a woman who worked a second job at a lawn and garden store because she loves landscaping and has a passion for sharing her knowledge. I know people who love doing handy work, so they work at Home Depot sharing their knowledge with others who share their passion for home repair. Get out there and turn your passion into another stream of income.

Start Your Own Business

People have this idea that if you are starting a business, it has to be some huge operation. That is not the case at all. Most big businesses started out as part-time businesses. If there is something you are passionate about, consider turning it into a business. Another guy who used to work at my company loved landscaping. He was passionate about the technical aspects of pruning and mowing. He spent a lot of his free time perfecting his yard. One day, he decided to start a landscaping business. He bought some equipment and went out on the weekend perfecting others' yards. As the demand soared for his services, he hired a couple of guys and got licensed and insured. He continued to work his day job, and he worked his side business in the evenings and on weekends. Today, he has a full-time operation that has expanded to several employees.

A guy who occasionally does some handiwork for me was once a bored employee in the corporate world. He fought through traffic and sat in a cubicle like many of us do today. He loved to do handiwork and carpentry, so he started doing work for friends on the weekend. He charged a fair price and did an excellent job. Soon word of mouth spread, and he had enough demand for his services that he quit his job to do carpentry and handiwork full-time. Now, he has a couple of guys who work with him. He found his way out of the monotony of corporate life, doing what he loved to do. Today, he is a small business owner.

Whether you are a full or part-time business owner, owning a business not only puts you in position to do what you really want to do, but it opens you up to several opportunities for additional streams of revenue. The guy who started his handiwork business talks to real estate entrepreneurs everyday who offer him opportunities to invest. The landscape business owner has found several opportunities to invest in other businesses and real estate.

Residual Income

I was always intrigued by the recurring income model. I would watch television shows that highlighted actors, singers, and musicians who had one hit their entire career, but the checks kept coming long after the television show or album stopped being popular or the TV show went off the air. I think about the author who writes a hit novel. For generations, he and his family collect royalty checks. The reason these people continue to make money is that they receive residuals for their work. Whenever someone uses or purchases a copy of their work, they are paid some percentage of the purchase. I cannot sing and dance. I have never acted in my life. So how could I receive residual income?

After spending some time thinking about it, I realized that real estate was the closest thing to residual income I could think of. Rental property excites me because you make a one-time investment. Instead of time, energy, and talent like performers, the real estate entrepreneur invests money. For example, I rented out the home where my family once lived. The monthly mortgage payment with insurance and taxes is about $1,000. The rent is $1,250. Therefore, as long as my tenant stays, I receive a residual of $250 every month. That does not include the tax deductions, the principal paid on the home loan, and appreciation. What a great stream of income! I increased my salary by $250 per month and it only gets better because as demand increases, my rent prices will increase, but my mortgage will stay the same. The tenant is paying my debt on an appreciating asset; plus the taxes and interest are tax deductible.

> Success breeds success, and streams of income breed more streams of income.

After all of that, I am walking away with the equivalent to a residual check. That extra $250 can be invested or added to my debt ladder to reduce my debt faster, while I still receive appreciation and equity. Thank you, Mr. Tenant!

Now, imagine having five or even ten rental properties. Your budget looks completely different now. You have created multiple streams of income for you and your family. That money you receive every month is no different than the actor who gets a residual check every time a show in which he made an appearance is aired. The only difference is that your residual income from rental properties is more predictable.

Success breeds success, and streams of income breed more streams of income. The concept of multiple streams of income is powerful. When I was struggling financially and looked at my budget, I felt sick. I had to deny myself so many things I enjoyed to keep within my budget. My investing power was limited, and when I did the math, it seemed as if it would take me two lifetimes to come close to approaching my goals. When I discovered the power of multiple streams of income, I could sit down and have a much larger number at the top of my budget worksheet. That provided me with flexibility and freedom in my financial life. Even an extra $250–$300 per month can really make a difference. The encouraging news is that those dollars are out there, and it doesn't take any special skill or super human power to create multiple streams of income. It only requires your doing a little homework. Focus on ways to leverage what you enjoy doing, and make it happen. There is a huge opportunity cost for doing nothing.

No matter what your skills are, there are opportunities out there for you to create multiple streams of income. The obvious ones are the common investment vehicles like mutual funds, 401(k)s, stocks, and bonds. Those should be taken advantage of no matter what else you decide to do. The other opportunities are right before your eyes. Assess your skills. Think about your hobbies. Now, think of creative ways those hobbies and skills can create income above and beyond your primary income. Figure out how much time you really have to explore these opportunities, and test the waters. You have nothing to lose. What you have to gain is real cash that becomes part of your budget. This real cash can help retire your debt or increase your investments, which in turn increases your income from sources other than your main salary.

If you grasp the concept of multiple streams of income, you will accelerate toward your goal. Think back to the asset discussion earlier in the book. In that section, we determined that at a modest 10% increase per year, a $250 per month investment would become a million dollars in about forty years. If your other streams of income contribute another $500 to your monthly investments, you will reach a million dollars in twenty-six years. If you invest more money, you will get there even faster. Revisit your goals and your budget. Determine how much more cash per month you need to get to your goals faster. Now, find those other streams of income and create a plan to make it happen.

Review

1. Focus on creating multiple streams of revenue. It will accelerate your financial growth.

2. Take advantage of the other streams of income that are easy to establish. Find investment vehicles like 401(k)s, mutual funds, and bonds. Do not leave money on the table by neglecting to collect the free money your employer and the government offer you.

3. Find another income stream in your hobbies and other activities outside of work. There are several ways to capitalize on your interests.

4. If you have the time, find a fun, part-time play job. That additional money will go a long way in helping you accomplish your dreams.

5. Turn your hobby and passion into a business. You can start a part-time home business tomorrow. Running a business of any size opens you up to other income opportunity streams.

6. Be a rock star, today. Residual income can provide you with a recurring revenue stream similar to actors and musicians.

7. Searching for multiple streams of revenue will open your mind to other possibilities. It can set you on a path toward your true calling in life, bring passion to your work, and get you to your goal faster.

Continuing the Lesson

Study these Scriptures to understand God's perspective on work and creating abundance.

Proverbs 21:5
The plans of the diligent lead to profit as surely as haste leads to poverty.

Proverbs 14:23
All hard work brings a profit, but mere talk leads only to poverty.

Psalm 90:17
May the favor of the Lord our God rest upon us; establish the work of our hands for us—yes, establish the work of our hands.

A Home is
More Than a Castle

"Home is the most popular, and will be the most enduring of
all earthly establishments."

Channing Pollock

One day I had my taxes done at H&R Block, and I walked out of their office stunned. I felt like I had been mugged. After forcing the tax consultant to recalculate my taxes over and over again, I realized that the results were not wrong. I owed $2,500 in taxes. I thought that it had to be a mistake. I was only making about $45,000 a year at the time. How could I possibly owe taxes?

I sat at my desk in my little apartment trying to figure out what had gone wrong. I was also trying hard to figure out how I would get the money to send to the IRS. Somehow this just did not seem fair. Later in the week, I went to my parents' house for some guidance. I sat down with my father and explained my dilemma to him. Still stunned, I looked at my dad and said, "I can't believe I owe IRS $2,500. It doesn't make sense!"

"You owe taxes because you do not own anything that would give you a tax break. If you owned a home, you would be able to write off the interest. That alone would put you in position to get a refund."

"I was thinking about owning a home, but that is a big step. I have been renting my entire adult life."

"A home is more than a castle. A home is like a mutual fund that keeps growing. You also get great tax benefits. You have excellent credit. Why would you be paying rent when you could be paying the same amount, owning an appreciating asset and getting tax relief?"

"I really need to look into that. I can't continue to pay taxes every year on my salary."

"The foundation of our family's financial success comes from your mom and me buying our first house. We purchased our first house using a VA loan, so we did not have to put any money down. When we moved, we had enough money to put down on our next home with plenty left over. Every time we moved to another house, we experienced the same thing. Between the appreciation of those homes and the tax breaks we got from being homeowners, we were able to move up in the world financially."

A home is more than a castle after all. Homes are the largest investment most people have. Homes generally increase in value as you pay down the interest, so they act as a personal mutual fund. Furthermore, the government encourages homeownership. When we buy homes, we contribute to the economy by buying appliances, furniture and other durable goods. These purchases boost the economy, and the equity in homes serves as a safety net for many families. Home equity provides owners with the ability to draw money out of the home in emergency situations. It is better for the government if you have your own safety net rather

> A home is more than a castle. A home is like a mutual fund that keeps growing.

than burden the welfare system. For those reasons and several others, the government gives you incentives to buy a home. Those incentives come in the form of tax deductions.

Homeownership is important for a lot of intangible reasons too. It gives you a secure place to raise your family. It provides a comfortable place where you can create family memories. A home is a rallying point for your family. Some of my fondest family memories took place at my grandmother's house. My aunts, uncles, and cousins would go there on Sundays and holidays to eat and fellowship. I have thirty years of memories in that house. My aunts and uncles have a lifetime of memories there. That home has brought stability and a sense of familiarity to three generations of my family.

God wants us to have families, and He expects us to provide them an inheritance. When Moses sought God's counsel on giving property to Zelophehad's daughters, God said:

> *What Zelophehad's daughters are saying is right. You must certainly give them property as an inheritance among their father's relatives and turn their father's inheritance over to them (Numbers 27:7).*

Additionally, if you want to be a part of a community, nothing builds community like homeownership. The other homeowners in your community have a vested interest in their property value, so they will make sure that certain standards are maintained. Homeowners pressure schools to be better because they have a vested interest in their children's education. Homeownership and community work together on so many different levels that it only makes sense that the government would give us an incentive to buy.

Buying a home is not nearly as complicated a transaction as you might think. You borrow money from a bank to purchase the home at a fixed or variable interest rate. You make a down payment, which gives the bank some money up front in case you default on the loan. You assume ownership of the loan, and you pay the loan off monthly. The monthly payment is a combination of the interest payment, principle, taxes, and insurance.

That is the Cliffs Notes version of a home purchase. There have been entire books written on this topic. In this chapter, I will introduce you to the basics of homeownership, so you can take that incremental leap toward homeownership.

Step One: Know What You Want

The first step to buying a home is to know what type of home you want. You need to know how much house you need or want, and you must know the resources available to you to make the purchase. When I purchased my first home, I was single. I only needed enough space for my dog, Troy, and me. So I did my research and determined that a condo fit my needs. In a condo, I would not have to do any major home repairs or yard work, and I only needed two bedrooms and one or two bathrooms.

Step Two: Find a Good Realtor

Find a good realtor. A good realtor makes all the difference in the world, especially on a first home purchase. I found my first realtor by walking into a real estate office near my apartment. She was horrible. This woman showed me the most rundown condos in the area. All of them were in bad locations and considerably less than I could afford.

I later found a better realtor who listened to me. She first took some financial information from me. An in-house lender ran my credit and explained how much of a home loan I qualified for based on my income, credit, and savings. I qualified for $110,000. The lender also provided me with an estimate of what my monthly mortgage payment and down payment would be on that loan. Now,

I had two pieces of information necessary to look for a home. I knew the type of home I wanted, and I knew how much I could borrow to make the purchase.

My realtor showed me places that fit my needs. She showed me this great condo on the third floor with two bedrooms, two bathrooms, a fireplace, and a deck. The asking price was close to, but less than my qualifying number. She knew the first rule of real estate investing—location, location, location. My agent knew the area well and understood which neighborhoods were popular.

She worked through the numbers with me and answered all of my questions. I was concerned about the down payment. I had just paid a huge tax bill. I asked her about the VA program, and she got all of the information I needed. Since I was an Army veteran in good standing, I qualified for a VA loan, which paid all of my down payment.

Step Three: Make an Offer

Now that I had found the place I wanted, my realtor explained my options for making an offer in detail. We discussed the items I wanted as part of the deal, like the refrigerator. She also went through contingencies such as inspection criteria. We then filled out an offer sheet and faxed it to the real estate agent for the seller (selling agent). After making an offer and receiving a counter offer from the seller, we came to an agreement on the purchase.

In order to prove that you are serious about the purchase, you must put down earnest money. Earnest money is money that you give the seller to show your commitment to making the deal. The earnest money is applied to your down payment or closing costs. If you renege on the deal, the seller keeps the money.

Step Four: Get the Property Inspected

Although an agreement was reached, we made the purchase contingent on the condo passing inspection. Buyers hire an inspector of their choice. The inspector thoroughly examined my potential new home for any flaws and structural problems. He documented all of the problem areas and gave me a written report. I sat down with my agent to determine the list of problems we wanted the buyer to fix. The seller refused to fix some items. Those items became bargaining chips. We asked the seller to either reduce the price or give me a check to pay for the repairs at the closing. Typically, the buyer and seller come to some happy medium. In my case, we did.

Step Five: Get a Loan

Now that I knew the agreed upon price, I worked with the lender in my realtor's office to finalize the loan paperwork. The lender provided me with a good-faith estimate. The good-faith estimate itemizes all of your closing costs. It also shows you the rate you will pay and your monthly mortgage payment.

An appraiser goes to the property to determine its value. If the value of the property meets or exceeds the offer, the lender will move forward to closing. In the rare case that the appraisal is less than the offer, the bank will have to re-examine the deal. The lender runs a risk of losing money by loaning you more money than the home is worth. If the home value matches the appraisal, then the bank has something of equal value to hold as collateral for the loan. Unless there is a major problem with the property, most appraisals are in line with the offering price.

Step Six: Prepare for Closing

I was all set to close on the condo after the appraisal, insurance, and the loan paperwork went through. I was so excited. After this month-long process, I was going to finally be a homeowner. But I did not understand the concept of closing costs. Closing costs are costs associated with filing the legal paperwork, taxes, and the mortgage for the remainder of the month after you close, and the mortgage payment for the following month. The day before closing my realtor told me to make sure I had a cashiers check for $3,250 for closing costs. I thought the VA loan covered that, but I was mistaken. So, I scrambled to scrape together the money for the closing.

Step Seven: Close the Deal

The closing takes place at the law firm that handles the paperwork. The seller and the buyer sit in a conference room and sign all of the legal documents required to transfer ownership to you; pay the seller; and pay the up-front costs to the lender. After about thirty minutes of signing papers, the realtors got their commission checks; the seller got his check for the difference between the selling price and the amount remaining on his loan; and I got keys to my new home. It was not nearly as difficult as I thought. One of my fondest memories is sitting on the floor in my new home the night after closing and celebrating with a pizza in a room full of boxes.

Great Decision

Buying a home was one of the best decisions I ever made. I was paying just a little more than I paid for rent, and my condo was twice the size of my apartment. I owned an appreciating asset, and I got a great tax break. After living in that condo for three years, I sold it just before I got married. I made enough money from selling the condo to make a down payment on a new house, pay for our honeymoon, and still had enough left to pay off some other debts. I could not believe that I had waited as long as I did to make the move to homeownership.

Foresight and Financing Options

Even after I closed on the condo, I was a little confused about what I had experienced. When I made my next home purchase, there were some things that became clearer to me, particularly with regard to financing. I took out a thirty-year fixed mortgage. A thirty-year fixed mortgage means that you are borrowing money at a set interest rate for thirty years. The payments are set, and the interest rate is fixed over those thirty years. I did not understand that *fixed* meant that only the interest rate was fixed. I later found out that the payments might not stay the same. Increases in insurance and property taxes will increase your monthly payments.

I decided to go with the thirty-year fixed mortgage because I was averse to risk. I thought that interest rates could climb on an adjustable rate mortgage (ARM), and I liked the security of knowing that my rate would stay the same. In retrospect, I should have known that being a single guy in my mid twenties meant my life would change dramatically over the next few years. If I got married and had a family, we surely would not have stayed in that condo. Even if I didn't get married in the next three to five years, I should have anticipated that my needs would change pretty quickly.

If I had knowledge and foresight, I would have gotten an adjustable rate mortgage (ARM). Adjustable rate mortgages are set at a lower interest rate than fixed mortgages, but your payments will vary over time. ARMs usually have an initial fixed rate period followed by adjustment intervals. Lenders offer several types of ARMs. The typical products are 3/1, 5/1, and 7/1.

With a 5/1 ARM, you pay a fixed interest rate for the first five years. After that, your interest rate is set for one year, every year following the fixed period. For example, you might have an ARM at a 5% annual percentage rate (APR) for five years. You will pay that rate for five years. At the end of the five years, the market sets your interest rate at 6.5%. So for the next 12 months, you pay 6.5%. The next year the market will determine your rate for the next year and so on. The 3/1 and 7/1 products work the same way except the fixed period is three or seven years.

Typically, people refinance their homes if they plan on staying past the fixed rate term. Refinancing a home simply means that you get a new loan with different terms to cover the remaining balance owed on the house. People use this tactic to either lower their payment or to cash out the equity in their homes. The only catch in refinancing over and over is that you will have to pay closing costs every time you refinance (typically 3% of the loan value).

Another financing option allows you to make a balloon payment at the end of the loan period. This option allows you to borrow at a set interest rate over a period of three, five, or seven years. At the end of the fixed period, the lender wants you to pay the full amount of the loan. At that point, people often refinance or sell the home.

These products and several others were available to me. However, I did not clearly understand my options with regard to financing the condo. Although I could have had a much lower rate, I still made a nice profit after only three years. Imagine if I had done my homework. If I had taken advantage of an ARM and paid 5% instead of 7.25%, my payments would have been lower, and I could have applied that extra money to my debts or investments.

Government Help

As I mentioned before, the government wants you to own a home. They realize that not everyone has the money to make a down payment and pay closing costs, so they put programs in place to assist homebuyers in purchasing a home. The programs the government offers are great deals. If you think you cannot afford the up-front cash to buy a home, go to a realtor and look into these programs.

There are two programs that come to mind immediately—VA and FHA. Both my father and I purchased our first homes with a VA loan. If you are a veteran who was discharged under favorable conditions, you probably qualify for a VA loan. The Veteran's Administration helps you purchase a home for personal use by paying the down payment. These loans are insured by the VA, which means the government promises to pay the lender if you default on the loan. The maximum for a VA home loan changes from year to year. As of 2005, you could get a VA loan for up to $359,650. You need to find a lender who is VA qualified, and then go to your nearest VA loan office to fill out some paperwork. It is that simple.

The Department of Housing and Urban Development (HUD) has programs available for homebuyers too. These Fair Housing Assistance (FHA) loans allow home-buyers with good credit to purchase homes by making a 3% down payment and including the closing costs in the mortgage. These programs are intended for low to middle-income buyers. The prospective buyer has to apply to a HUD approved lender. Then, the buyer finds a HUD home that they want to purchase.

> No matter how much cash you have or whether you have good credit or not, go talk to a realtor today to find out what your options are.

At that point, they make an offer. There is an offer period, and the highest reasonable bid is accepted.

There are similar programs like the Nehemiah program. This program also assists home buyers in making a down payment on a home. This program has specific homes listed throughout the country. The program provides 6% toward the down payment and/or closing costs. You can visit www.getdownpayment.com for more information.

If you really want to purchase a home, but do not have the cash to cover the down payment and closing costs, these government-sponsored loans are a great opportunity to enjoy the benefits of homeownership. Even if your credit is not good, there are HUD-approved loans insured for special credit risks. If you want to own a home, no matter how much cash you have or whether you have good credit or not, go talk to a realtor today to find out what your options are.

Purchasing Your Dream Home

A good friend of mine wants to purchase a home for about $150,000. She does not know where to start. Since I was in the same situation seven years ago, I want to use this as an opportunity to lay the groundwork for making that $150,000 home a reality for her.

First, you must understand the math of homeownership. Your mortgage payment consists of interest, principal, and escrow. The interest is the finance charge for borrowing the money. It is the same as the finance charge you pay on credit cards. The principal is the money that goes toward actually paying down the loan. The more you pay above your set mortgage payment, the less interest you pay, and the more money is applied against the principal to actually retire your loan. Escrow is money that the lender puts aside to pay insurance and taxes. If the lender underestimates the escrow amount or you receive a significant increase in property taxes, they will increase your escrow payments the following year to make up for the shortfall. If they overestimate the escrow amount, they will refund the money to you.

Now, you must determine what you need to make the purchase. If the home you want to buy costs $150,000, you will need 5% down unless you qualify for some special mortgage deal through VA or FHA. You will also need about 3% of the loan value for closing. Then, you have to make sure you can qualify for the loan. A one-hour visit to a real estate office will confirm how much the lender will loan you. Next, you need to make sure that you can make the monthly payments. As a rule of thumb, your mortgage payment will be $6 for every thousand dollars of home loan.

Let's figure out what my friend will have to do to get into her $150,000 home.

Home Price	$ 150,000.00
Down Payment = $ 150,000 x .05 (5%)	$7,500.00
Loan Amount = $ 150,000 – $7,500	$142,500.00
Closing Cost = $ 142,500 x .03 (3%)	$4,275.00
Amount Due at Closing = $ 7,500 + $4,275	$11,775.00
Estimated Monthly Mortgage = $ 142,500/$1,000 x $6	$855.00

If my friend has $11,775, she can go out and buy a house today. She might also be able to buy a house today with $7,500. She can work out a deal with the seller to pay closing costs and roll it into the purchase price. The bank can also add a fraction of the loan amount (called *points*) to her loan to cover the closing cost. She must make sure that the additional percentage points do not exceed what she would can afford to pay. Any additional costs that are added to her loan amount will increase her loan balance and monthly payments.

That is a quick summary of the math involved in home buying. There are more details, but that is the gist of how the math flows in that transaction. Now, let's examine how the math can work in her favor. Let's say my friend now owns this $150,000 home. She financed $142,750 using a 5/1 ARM at 4.29%. Her payments have been $705.59 for five years. The home appreciates at a modest rate of 7% per year. She lived in the home for five years, and now she is getting married and moving. After five years, her loan balance would be $129,467.

If the home appreciates 7% per year, the value of the home will be $210,381 after five years. The math would flow as follows:

Value of Home at Year 5	$ 210,381.00
Amount Remaining on the Loan	−129,467.00
Gross from the Sale ($210,381 − $129,467)	$ 80,914.00
Real Estate Agents' Commission at 6% of selling price ($210,381 x .06)	−12,622.86
Net Profit ($80,914.32 − $12,622.86)	$ 68,291.14

That is not bad at all! After subtracting the $4,275 in closing costs from her original purchase, she will have made $64,016.14. This is the power of homeownership. She also will have gotten a tax break over the five years she owned the house. She will have owned an appreciating asset, and she will have had a better place to come home to for five years. Today, she is paying $800 a month to rent a small apartment. If she continues living there for five years, she will pay $48,000 with nothing to show for it. That is a difference of over $100,000, not including the tax deductions ($64,016.14 profit − $7,500 down payment + $48,000 rent = $104,516.14).

Let's go back to the credit discussion for a moment. If her credit is bad, she will not qualify for the loan. If her credit is so-so, she could qualify for the loan, but at a higher rate. Let's say that her shaky credit added 3% to the loan. Her monthly payment would be $977.68 per month. That's over $200 more per month than she would have paid with good credit. Her principal balance on the same loan over five years would be $134,622.14. That's over $5,000 more than her balance would be with good credit.

I encourage you to take the time to do the math and explore your possibilities. There are great websites like www.bankrate.com and others that have mortgage calculators that will tell you what your monthly payments will be for various loans. Every day that you rent is a losing proposition. Think about the opportunity cost for inaction. Within five years, the same person has added over $100,000 to her financial scorecard by taking an incremental leap of faith. You can too.

Purchasing Rental Homes

I do not want to spend too much time on this, but I feel that it is important to mention. In the case study we did for my friend, she bought a place, and lived there for five years. She then sold the property and walked away with over $68,000. Do you remember my friend Doug Keipper whom I talked about in the chapter on vision? Doug took the concept of homeownership to another level. The exact same concepts I described to you regarding buying your first house are identical to what you would do for a rental property. The only difference is that with a rental property someone else pays your mortgage for you!

I want you to understand this concept. You take the risk of paying the down payment and the closing costs. Then, you advertise the home (another risk). You find a tenant (another risk). You have the tenant sign a contract that you can get from any office supply store. Now, you are a landlord. It is that easy. The bottom line is that you take the up-front risk. You find the tenant, and the tenant pays the mortgage for you. Those payments we discussed earlier—interest, escrow, and principal—are completely paid by the tenant; plus you get an extra couple of hundred dollars per month for taking the risk.

You can do this over and over. Doug has visions of doing it twenty times. The only barrier to entry is poor credit. Reread the credit chapter. It is important that you are considered trustworthy. If you are deemed trustworthy, you can access money all day long to make investments in appreciating assets that other people finance. Think about it. If banks trust me, I can literally play Monopoly.

Some of you might be wondering, "How can you just keep getting more money?" First, with excellent credit, the lender knows I am trustworthy. As long as I have a signed lease to prove that I have tenants who are carrying my mortgage risk, the lender will loan me more money. Also, those rental properties have equity in them, so the lender knows that I can use that equity to pay them back if necessary. Although the total dollar figure in loans is high, my tenants paying my other mortgages, my excellent credit, and the equity in those properties make it easy for me to borrow more.

Now, think about the chapter on vision. Can you see it now? You understand the process. You put into place the financial discipline explained in this book. You start to see your debt go down, and your credit score increase. Then, you see your savings and investments go up. Soon you have the courage to take the incremental leap to purchase your first home. After you experience the joy of homeownership, you will see that it is not rocket science. Then, you figure out that you can do this all day long, so why not make money from doing this. Therein is the path to your vision.

Homeownership is one of the many things that make America great. I was hesitant about writing a chapter on homeownership, but homeownership is important. Homeownership creates the foundation for family wealth. If you have a family, and you do not own a home, you are missing out. Like 401(k)s that employers match, homeownership is free money. You would be foolish not to find a way to do it.

Get in the game and participate. There are great professionals out there who can help you buy your first home. Make the incremental leap to talk to a real estate agent and lender today. If you are skeptical of their claims, get online. Go to www.google.com and do a search on "home mortgage." You will find more information than you can possibly remember. Agents know the Internet gives you the power to keep them honest, so most are above board. If you ever question anything your agent or lender tells you, go online and check it out, or ask a knowledgeable friend or family member.

Home ownership boomed after World War II. GIs returned home looking to make up for lost time. They married the sweethearts they left behind when they went off to war. They had several children (now known as the Baby Boomers), so the government decided to make it easier for these war heroes to have a home. They created programs that gave benefits to veterans so they could experience homeownership. Since then homeownership has been a right of passage for every American. Homes are memories. Homes are security. Homes are equity to help us in troubled times. Homes are absolutely more than castles.

Review

1. Home ownership can set the foundation for your financial future.

2. A home has intangible value like memories and stability for your family.

3. Home ownership is not as difficult as you might think.

4. Home ownership can make you much better off than renting.

5. Take the first step of homeownership. Talk to a reputable real estate agent, and find out if you are a candidate to buy a home today.

6. Small victories add up to major wins. The small step of buying your first home can stoke the flames for a vision of owning several properties.

7. Home ownership is the American way. It can help protect your family in hard times and lift them up in good times. Whether you are male or female, take the lead and move your family toward homeownership.

Continuing the Lesson

Study these Scriptures regarding homeownership.

Psalm 84:3–4

[3]Even the sparrow has found a home, and the swallow a nest for herself, where she may have her young—a place near your altar, O Lord Almighty, my King and my God. [4]Blessed are those who dwell in your house; they are ever praising you.

Numbers 27:6–11

[6]And the LORD said to him, [7]"What Zelophehad's daughters are saying is right. You must certainly give them property as an inheritance among their father's relatives and turn their father's inheritance over to them. [8]Say to the Israelites, 'If a man dies and leaves no son, turn his inheritance over to his daughter. [9]If he has no daughter, give his inheritance to his brothers. [10]If he has no brothers, give his inheritance to his father's brothers. [11]If his father had no brothers, give his inheritance to the nearest relative in his clan, that he may possess it. This is to be a legal requirement for the Israelites, as the LORD commanded Moses.'"

Lesson 10

Create a Comprehensive Plan

"Have a good plan, execute it violently, and do it today."

Douglas MacArthur

One day, my dad was on his way back from a charity event, and he met me for lunch. We discussed the typical subjects like family, friends, and sports. Eventually, we discussed my personal finances. As we talked, I told him about some of my success. We looked back to just a few years back and recalled what a mess my financial life was then.

My dad flashed a proud smile from across the table, "All of the lessons I have taught you did not mean that much if taken individually. You had to take all that I have taught you, and make a comprehensive plan for success."

"So, these conversations have been lessons all along?"

"Yes, they have been lessons about life and personal finances. But they are more. These lessons have been about stewardship and accountability. If you can be accountable, you can be a leader. As the head of your household, you have to be a leader."

"So what are you suggesting?"

"I am suggesting that you go home and think about the lessons I have taught you over the years. Most of them you grasped, and others you pushed aside. But take these important lessons to heart. Continue to create and adjust your comprehensive plan for your life, and be disciplined enough to see it through."

I really enjoyed my conversations with my father. The funny thing is that I never really knew that I was being taught anything. As far as I was concerned, we were just talking, but my father works on a whole different level. What was a normal conversation for me was teaching for him. I got his message, and I sat down one evening and sorted through all that I had learned to put together a plan for my life.

Step One: Seek God's Guidance

Spend time in prayer before you embark on your journey of financial success. Ask the Lord for wisdom and discipline. Ask God to open your eyes to the possibilities. He has a plan for all of us. By seeking Him, He will give you peace about your mission. In seeking the Lord in prayer, He will open you up to the abundance He has for all of us. Throughout the process, continue to pray.

In prayer, we get to know who God is for ourselves. Your friends are your friends because you spent time with them. You got to know them through their actions and your conversations. I encourage you to do the same with God. As you get to know Him, you will see the value in being obedient in the form of tithing. When you decide to tithe, ask God for the faith and discipline to continue that obedience. Giving opens a circle of abundant blessings for you and others. Commit to tithing, and you will take the first steps to abundance.

Step Two: Create a Vision

Read newspaper articles. Read the books that I have recommended in this book, and think about your vision for life. Consider all the things that you do well and the things that you do not do well. Dream about where you would like to be in ten years and do not censor that dream.

If you are married, sit down with your spouse and dream together. Think about what you would both like to do and make a plan for the future. When you do, put it down on paper. Whether you are single or married, the work begins once you have established a plan.

Discuss your dreams. If you are married, talk to your spouse about your collective goals and the vision you have for your family. If you are single, discuss your goals with like-minded people, friends, and family. When you discuss your goals and dreams, you can't help but talk about how you are going to accomplish them. The power of discussion also helps you find motivation in others who are striving to attain their own goals and dreams. Others who are striving to reach their goals can often help you through shared knowledge, connections, and encouragement.

Wrap your mind around your goals. When you present a problem to yourself, you cannot help but think of ways to solve that problem. If you have a burning desire to fulfill your dreams, you will do whatever is necessary to achieve them.

Now that you have written your plan on paper, determine what it will take to make that plan a reality. My wife and I dream of having two homes—a home in Atlanta and a vacation home near the beach. We know how much it will cost to accomplish that dream. We also dream about what we really want to do. My wife wants to have children and run a successful psychology practice. I want to write, teach, and start a small business. We also have a long-term vision of our children having the freedom to pursue their passions without worrying about money. Most importantly, we have spiritual goals of being major contributors to ministries that support people in third-world countries. We also have dreams of having our own charitable foundation.

Today, we are still working toward our goals, but we can see them. We have a plan in place to accomplish them. We just need the strength and discipline to stick to it. That strength and discipline comes from God. God's strength and guidance is empowering, and it can help you gain control of your financial life.

In order to accomplish our goals, we know what we need to do financially. Every decision we make revolves around our collective dream. We know how much we have invested. We know how much money we have in mutual funds, and we are pushing everyday to reach our dream. The bottom line is that you cannot push for a goal that is not conceived. Once you conceive the dream, you now have the vision to make it happen.

Know where you want to go. This is where vision comes into play. Think hard about what you want. Where do you want to be in one, two, five, and ten years? What type of lifestyle do you want to lead? What do you want to be doing for a living in the future? What kind of life do you want for your children? After you think about it in broad terms, write it down in specifics on paper.

Step Three: Know Where You Stand

There is a map at the mall that has a star on it that tells you where you are. If you are trying to get to Sears, you know how to get there based on the map. If you did not know where you were, you would wander aimlessly looking for your destination. Before you can move toward your vision, you must know where you stand financially.

Create a financial scorecard for yourself. Determine how much you have in your bank account. Find out how much you have invested in your 401(k), mutual funds, and stocks. If you have a home, check recent sales in your neighborhood to determine how much your home is worth. Calculate the value of all of your assets.

Now take out all of your bills, credit card statements, and mortgage statements. Add up how much you owe. That number will be your debt. Take your total assets and subtract your debt. That is your financial scorecard. Do you like what you see? Don't be discouraged if your net worth is low or negative. At least you know where you stand.

Go online or call Equifax to request your credit report. Know what your credit score is. If it is not good, take immediate action to improve it. If your credit is good, then you are in a good place. Either way, you need to know where you are from a credit perspective because credit plays an important part in accomplishing your financial goals.

Step Four: Set Specific Goals

Based on your financial scorecard, decide where you need to be to accomplish your goals in one, two, five and ten years. Now that you have your dreams on paper, and you know how much it takes to make your dream come true, take a minute to sample your dream. Literally cut out pictures of your dream. If it is a home on the beach, find a magazine, cut out a picture, and put it in a prominent place where you have to look at it often. Occasionally, go house hunting to see the house you will live in when you reach your goal.

In the short-term, make incremental, achievable goals and work hard to accomplish them. Remember that success breeds success, so set yourself up for success by making incremental leaps. Every small victory is one step closer to that grand vision you have created for yourself and your family.

Step Five: Commit to a Budget

You now know where you stand financially, today. You know what you have, and you know how much you owe. You should know how much you make. Determine what your take home pay is, and establish an attainable budget. Write down all of your expenses along the way so you see where your money is spent. This is a work in progress. You can make budgetary adjustments as you get a better feel for where you can reduce spending. You know how much you need to invest monthly to accomplish your goals. Go back to the budget guideline and work your number into the budget.

There are some places that will get a higher or lower percentage of your budget, but taxes and tithes are automatic. With what you have left, determine how you can adjust your lifestyle to live below your means. This will take some work and discipline, but you can do it. If you work through the spreadsheet and realize that the numbers exceed your budget, go back to your expense journal, and make some tough decisions about where to make cuts. Remember, it is impossible for you to accomplish your financial goals if you spend beyond what you earn. Budgeting is the anchor to your financial success.

Step Six: Work to Increase Your Financial Scorecard

Another part of knowing where you stand financially is knowing your financial scorecard. If you don't calculate the value of your assets and subtract the money you owe, you will not know where you are or how much it will take to get you where you want to go. Revisit your budget. Do your monthly investments and debt payments match your goals? If you hope to have a financial scorecard worth $500,000 in ten years, do the numbers in your budget suggest that you can make it?

Before going any further, visit www.bankrate.com. This website has a number of financial calculators. You can put in your monthly investment, and it will tell you how long it will take you to reach your goal. Play around with the numbers to understand how your monthly investment will affect the time it takes to reach your goals. Once you play around with the calculators, go back to your goals, and see if they are realistic, based on the numbers you saw using the calculator. Now go back to revisit your budget to determine the maximum you can invest.

After you complete that exercise, focus on the debt side of the scorecard. First, call your creditors and ask for a lower rate. Cancel any unnecessary credit cards. Take one low-interest credit card, put it in a plastic bag filled with water, and freeze it. Set up a debt ladder by writing down the totals you owe starting with the highest interest debt. Work your way down to the lowest. Look at the minimum payments and write that number down next to the names of the creditors. Check your budget for the amount allocated for debt payments. Add up the minimum payment from the lowest to the highest except for the highest interest debt. Subtract that figure from the debt entry in your budget. Apply the difference to the highest interest debt until it is paid off. Then, start working on the next highest interest. Continue doing this until your debt is gone.

Step Seven: Be Trustworthy

Make it a point to be a trustworthy person. See what creditors think of your trustworthiness by getting a credit report to see what your score is. Comb the credit report for any errors, and take aggressive action to correct any discrepancies. If your credit score is low, work to it by paying your bills on time and reducing your consumer debt. Being a trustworthy person is an important foundation for financial success. With good credit, you can borrow money for constructive debt at a much lower interest rate. Good credit allows you access to money that people with bad credit can never get. The opportunity cost of being untrustworthy is steep!

Step Eight: Maximize Your Investments

First, give yourself a raise. If you work for a company with 401(k) benefits, at minimum, invest the maximum amount your company will match. That is effectively giving yourself a pay raise. Take advantage of the free money out there. It does not make sense to leave that money on the table.

There is more free money to be had from the government. Take advantage of the Roth IRA. Determine the maximum you can invest in a Roth based on your income, and put in the maximum. Roth investments grow tax free, so when you reach retirement age you will not have to pay tax on the capital gains. That means that at retirement age, you can take money out and not be taxed at all. This is a fantastic deal!

Make sound investments. Whether it is in a 401(k), Roth or non-retirement mutual fund, invest consistently in a reputable fund that has a track record of sustained growth. Do not move money around whenever the market hiccups. Stay the course. Keep investing every month, and let dollar cost averaging work for you.

Step Nine: Find Multiple Streams of Income

We operate as if we can only hold one job, but there are multiple streams of income out there for all of us. Most of us have more time on our hands than we think. This extra time gives us the opportunity to make extra cash while doing the hobbies we love to do. If you go back to your budget, figure out how much an extra $500 per month will impact you. Run that extra $500 through the calculators you played around with earlier. Do the math to see how much faster your debt is paid off if you made payments of $500 more per month. You will be surprised at how quickly your finance charges decrease and, consequently, how fast you retire that debt.

Investments in homes and mutual funds are another stream of income that will boost your financial scorecard. Develop residual income that will make money for you years to come. Work to consistently increase your investment in appreciating assets, and your financial scorecard will grow quickly.

Step Ten: Regularly Check the Map

As you apply these principles, check monthly to see how your actions have improved your financial scorecard. Get inspiration from your hard work and discipline by seeing your progress in black and white. When I first started following these lessons my father taught me, my goals were fairly limited, but a few things happened along the way. I got consistent pay increases. My property value increased more than I expected, and I found new ways to reduce my expenses. Also, interest rates went down considerably which opened up new possibilities for me.

As these events occurred, I revisited my budget and my goals. My short-term goal was to live in a larger home. When interest rates dipped and I received a raise, buying that larger home was actually only a couple hundred dollars more a month than my much smaller home. Then, I decided to keep my smaller home, and I turned it into a rental property. My goals shifted significantly. I found another stream of income from an appreciating asset. My new goal became to acquire another rental property. My goal of owning a large home in three years turned into owning a larger home and two rental properties. My original map was no good to me anymore.

I would never have made it to the place I am today if I had not constantly checked my map. When I realized that I was at a place where I could accelerate my financial scorecard growth, I took advantage of it. Without knowing where I stood or where I wanted to go, I could never have made the moves that I made. I encourage you to get serious about your financial destiny. Follow these steps, and consistently check your progress against your goals. When you wrap your mind around where you want to go, you will find all kinds of creative ways to get there.

Review

1. Find peace through prayer and seeking God's wisdom before you start the important task of putting together a financial plan for yourself and your family.

2. Know where you stand. You cannot make goals without understanding where you stand today.

3. Dream. Think broadly about the possibilities, and make those goals real to you and your family.

4. Know where you want to go. That is half the battle. When you know where you want to go, you will be resourceful in finding a way to get there.

5. Budget. Determine a realistic budget. Continue to craft your budget to reduce expenses and increase investment in appreciating assets.

6. Focus on increasing your financial scorecard. Aggressively reduce debt and increase investments.

7. Be trustworthy. Your credit is a reflection of who you are.

8. Maximize your investments. There is free money out there to be had. Make sure you take advantage of it.

9. Find multiple streams of income. These streams are all around you. You just need to open your eyes to them.

10. Consistently check your map. This constant check will keep you on course and lead you to places of your dreams.

Continuing the Lesson

The virtuous woman in Proverbs 31 is a fitting ending study. The passage illustrates the comprehensive nature of godly financial management and planning. Here, we have a family earning and using wealth wisely. They are assets to their community and examples for all of us. Study this Scripture and outline how you will align your plan with the principles of this book.

Proverbs 31:10–31

[10]A wife of noble character who can find? She is worth far more than rubies. [11]Her husband has full confidence in her and lacks nothing of value. [12]She brings him good, not harm, all the days of her life. [13]She selects wool and flax and works with eager hands. [14]She is like the merchant ships, bringing her food from afar. [15]She gets up while it is still dark; she provides food for her family and portions for her servant girls. [16]She considers a field and buys it; out of her earnings she plants a vineyard. [17]She sets about her work vigorously; her arms are strong for her tasks. [18]She sees that her trading is profitable, and her lamp does not go out at night. [19]In her hand she holds the distaff and grasps the spindle with her fingers. [20]She opens her arms to the poor and extends her hands to the needy. [21]When it snows, she has no fear for her household; for all of them are clothed in scarlet. [22]She makes coverings for her bed; she is clothed in fine linen and purple. [23]Her husband is respected at the city gate, where he takes his seat among the elders of the land. [24]She makes linen garments and sells them, and supplies the merchants with sashes. [25]She is clothed with strength and dignity; she can laugh at the days to come. [26]She speaks with wisdom, and faithful instruction is on her tongue. [27]She watches over the affairs of her household and does not eat the bread of idleness. [28]Her children arise and call her blessed; her husband also, and he praises her: [29]"Many women do noble things, but you surpass them all." [30]Charm is deceptive, and beauty is fleeting; but a woman who

fears the LORD is to be praised. [31]Give her the reward she has earned, and let her works bring her praise at the city gate.

Conclusion

The lessons from my father taught me first and foremost to honor God with tithes and offerings; to seek His guidance and wisdom, and get to know Him. As I have grown to know God, he has opened my mind to abundance through giving. The love of money is the root of all evil. Love God with all your heart. Focus on maximizing your talent. Go forth and make money, but do not let the pursuit of money cloud your vision.

Have a vision for your future. No one else will create a vision for you. You know better than anyone else what your talents are. You know what you want to do and where you want to go. Take some time to explore your options. Know where you want to go, and be prepared to manage your personal finances to accomplish your end. Begin with the end in mind. Write it down in bold letters, and refer to it often. This is the motivation you will need to stay the course to accomplish your dreams.

The key to experiencing abundance is opening your mind and heart to giving. Tithing is simple obedience to God, but do not stop there. There are many excellent charities that need resources to help those who are less fortunate. Giving opens your mind to abundance, and the act of giving places you in a position to receive. Make a commitment to giving, and you will be surprised at the blessings, tangible and intangible, that you will receive. Wealth is empty if it is not shared.

You must keep score. Know where you stand. The only way you can possibly put together a plan for yourself and your family is to know where you are today and where you want to be tomorrow.

You cannot accomplish weight loss goals if you do not know what your weight is today and what you want your weight to be in the future. Know where you are and where you want to go, and then make a plan to accomplish your vision. Remember, you cannot do this unless you know the score. Know the score by developing a financial scorecard, and continually check the score.

Live below your means. If you cannot live below your means, you will never accomplish your vision. You will only go backwards. Living below your means starts with budgeting. Stick to your budget religiously. Continually look for ways to reduce expenses and adjust your budget frequently. There are many ways to reduce costs. Understand where money is wasted, and stop the wastefulness. Focus your resources on increasing your financial scorecard.

Invest without ceasing. Make it a point to invest even a little every month. Invest in appreciating assets like homes, mutual funds, stocks, bonds, 401(k)s, and IRAs. They will increase steadily in value, and help the asset side of your financial equation. Investing is the best way to provide yourself and your family a financial future. The more you invest, the more that money will work for you. It is like having a miniature version of you working away somewhere and producing income.

Stay clear of debt. The price of debt is high. It will keep you in bondage because it sucks up resources that could be spent on appreciating assets. Debt has a tremendous opportunity cost.

There are two types of debt—toxic and constructive debt. Toxic debt is used to buy depreciating assets like clothes and entertainment. Constructive debt is used to pay for college, homes, and businesses. Understand how both types of debt really affect you. Look at your finance charges, and think about what you could be doing with that money. Once you get serious about getting rid of debt, put a plan in place to:

- Prioritize payments using the debt ladder.
- Stop spending using credit cards,.

- Search for better rates.
- Consider consolidating your debt.

Take aggressive action with regard to debt. The finance charges you pay every month are robbing you of several years of your financial life.

Keep good credit. Having bad credit is expensive, and it limits your ability to borrow constructive debt at a low interest rate. When you have to borrow money at a high interest rate, it will cost you hundreds of dollars a month more than the person with good credit. There is a tremendous opportunity cost to being deemed untrustworthy. If you have good credit today, fight with every ounce of energy to maintain that good credit. If your credit is bad, do everything in your power to improve your credit. People do not realize how expensive it is to have bad credit. If you look at the added expense in terms of higher interest rates and estimate how much you could earn by investing those extra finance charges in an appreciating asset, you will quickly see just how expensive bad credit is. Take action today to get your credit straight.

Successful people develop multiple streams of income. You should do the same. Take advantage of the low hanging fruit. The 401(k)s, Roth IRAs, and mutual funds should be your first additional streams of income. You can give yourself a raise today by taking advantage of the free money that is out there. Explore your hobbies. There is a money-making opportunity in the activities you like to do outside of work. Consider starting a small business on the side doing something that you are passionate about. The more streams of income you develop, the more financial flexibility you have. Multiple streams of income keep you from being completely dependent on your employers. My challenge to you is to go find opportunities outside of work. You will be surprised how many ways you can earn money doing something you enjoy.

A home is more than a castle. A home is a foundation for prosperity. It is a place full of memories and intangibles. Home ownership is the American dream. Participate in the American dream today. You do not have to have tens of thousands of dollars in the bank. There are several programs that can get you into a home. Go talk to a realtor and get the facts. Understand what resources are available to you. Home buying is not a difficult transaction. A home is an appreciating asset that will boost your financial scorecard. Home ownership provides you with a place to call your own, appreciating value on your investment, and a tax deduction. Home ownership has been the foundation for wealth for millions of families. Get in the homeownership game today.

Now that you have all of this information, it is time to do something with it. Sit down alone or with your family and make a comprehensive plan. Pray for guidance and wisdom as you make decisions about your financial future. Dream about where you want to be. Formulate a vision of what you want to be doing, and how you want to live in the future. Write it down on paper. Determine where you stand today. How much are you worth compared to how much you need to be worth to fulfill your dreams? Create a budget, and take decisive action to eliminate things in your life that are a waste of money.

Attack debt and eliminate it as if it were a disease. Invest monthly in appreciating assets. Work to steadily increase your investments. Know where you stand from a credit standpoint. Credit is money. If you have bad credit, it will cost you. Work to improve your credit whether it is good or bad. It really does make a difference.

Money is fluid. The overall premise of money is: Hold to pay or pay to hold. The way to be financially successful is to maximize the opportunities for people to pay you to hold versus you paying banks and credit card companies to hold their cash.

If you follow these lessons from my father, you will maximize these opportunities and discover abundance. No one ever said that this was easy to do. There are all types of personal and psychological hurdles to overcome in order to achieve your goals. But if you truly see the value in being prosperous, make a decision to do something about it today.

I hope that you enjoyed reading this book as much as I have enjoyed writing it. I offer this book to those people who, like me, have struggled to grasp the concepts of personal finances. If you have not been exposed to personal finances, the goal of this book is to plant a seed that you will continue to nurture and grow. No matter what your salary is, you can practice good stewardship.

No matter how knowledgeable you are about personal finance, you will make mistakes. We are all human. All of us get off track from our goals from time to time. Today, my family still struggles with keeping within our budget. The important thing is to not stray too far off course. Do not give up if you make mistakes. Mastering personal finances is like mastering any other skill. It takes hard work and discipline to be great. Cut yourself some slack, but be diligent in your pursuit of your financial goals. You have to be genuinely motivated in order to succeed.

The way you handle your personal finances are a direct reflection of you. Your choices speak volumes about your generosity, discipline, self-esteem, and trustworthiness. If you possess those traits, demonstrate them through your stewardship of God's gifts.

If you didn't grasp any of the more technical discussion, make sure you understand these points:

- **Give God your tithe.** Tithing is a reflection of your faith and capacity to give. Tithing also opens your heart to giving and creates an abundance mentality.
- **Live below your means.** If you live below your means, you will stay out of debt.
- **Invest early and often.** You do not need to be a financial genius to identify a safe mutual fund and consistently contribute to it.

These three points alone will get you well on your way to achieving your goals. If you incorporate the other lessons in this book into your life, you will achieve financial success beyond your wildest dreams.

I encourage you to read more on personal finance. There are great books out there that elaborate on some of the points in this book. Other authors also give you a different angle on the same material that could be helpful to your growth. A healthy dose of motivational and personal finance books will help you complete the picture of success, and they will help you shape your vision. Some great books to read are *The Millionaire Next Door, The Word on Finances, The Seven Habits of Highly Effective People,* and *Keys to Success* are just a few (See Appendix B: Suggested Reading List for the authors). Also visit our website at www.hesaiditidioit.com.

If you seek God's guidance and wisdom, you cannot fail. Get to know Him, and your faith will take you where you need to go. That faith and a little knowledge will make a tremendous difference in your life. Life is not about money. Life is about making the most of the talents and resources God has provided you. Focus on your talents. Put those talents to work for you. It is important for your growth, and it is critical to the long-term financial health of your family.

My father taught me so many different lessons about personal finances and life. He said it, and I did it. I am eternally grateful for the wisdom that he and my mom have bestowed upon me. I am blessed to have godly parents. They seek to help me avoid some of their pitfalls in life and personal finances. These lessons from my father are truly lessons from the Father. God's blessings to my family come from wisdom that He instilled in my parents through rough times and disappointments. I hope and pray that this book enriched your lives literally and figuratively. May the lessons from my father also keep you from the same pitfalls in life's journey.

Charles W. Buffington III

Epilogue

This book was written to help ordinary, everyday people achieve financial freedom and pass a legacy of abundance to future generations. I am an ordinary, everyday person who reached the illusive goal of financial freedom through the lessons I learned from studying my Heavenly Father's Word, the Holy Bible.

Much of what you read in this book comes from my wife, Minnie's, and my experience in learning God's principles governing finances and trying to be obedient. Along the way, we made many mistakes; however, we did not dwell on the mistakes. We took the consequences, learned the lesson, and moved on toward our vision of financial freedom.

As you see by his testimony, my son, Charles III, has also embraced the lessons of the Father and is well on his quest for financial freedom. By learning and applying these timeless lessons, you, too, can be free. My prayer is that you will use this book as a guide to be a better steward of the finances that the Master has entrusted to your care.

The Bible says in John 10:10 that Jesus came that we might have life, and have it more abundantly. Jesus finished His work on the cross. He fulfilled His vision. Now, we must do our part. May God's richest blessings always be with you.

Yours in Christ,
Charles W. Buffington, Jr.

Appendix A: Personal Finance Facts

Facts About You and Your Money
from www.personalfinancemastery.com[10]

- The average American will SPEND $1,860,000 on goods and services in his or her lifetime.—*American Demographics*

- A baby-boomer who makes $50,000 a year today will need ONE MILLION DOLLARS in savings to replace that income by the time he or she retires. —*USA Today*

- The average cost of owning and operating a car over the course of a person's working life is estimated to be more than $200,000. —*American Institute for Economic Research*

- If the above costs of owning a car were cut in half (in other words each car was kept twice as long before replacement), the savings invested at 10% over the same person's working life would build up to an additional $1,317,495 in retirement income!

- An extra payment per month of $100 applied to a 9%, 30-year fixed $100,000 mortgage will save $75,394 in interest.

- Adding just 15% to your monthly mortgage payment can cut 10 to 15 years off the average mortgage.

- More than HALF of all the money you make in your lifetime will go toward taxes, debt payments, and fees.

- Average homeowners stay in their homes for 7.1 years [National Association of Realtors®]. With an average 8% mortgage, they will sell their homes still owing over 90% of the principal. If they continue this trend, they will NEVER pay off a home in their lifetimes!

---

10. Personal Finance Mastery, "Facts About You and Your Money," www.personalfinancemastery.com/v2/stats.htm (accessed April 27, 2005)

- The average 45 to 54-year old has just $2,600 in the bank. —*Capital Research Associates*

- The average savings of a retired couple is only $7,000.

- On average, Americans can expect to receive just 37% of the annual retirement income they will need to live comfortably. —*Oppenheimer Funds Dist., Inc.*

- Eighty-five percent (85%) of Americans have a true net worth of less than $250. —*Social Security Administration*

- Every day, over 2,200 Americans lose their jobs.

- Parents can expect to pay over $150,000 to raise a child to age 18; and if the child goes to college, add another $70,000 to $160,000.

Unprecedented numbers of Americans are in debt for record amounts.

- Fifty million credit cards are issued annually.

- Seventy percent (70%) of credit card holders carry a balance, which averages over $3,000.

- Payments on debt now account for 92% of family disposable income.

- Total consumer debt is over $5 trillion. That's about the same as the government's "national" debt everyone keeps talking about.

- Personal bankruptcies are at an all-time high of about a million a year.

Banks, finance, and credit card companies have encouraged indebtedness.

- Credit card companies are marketing to college students, so the borrowing habit begins in the earliest stages of adulthood.

- Credit cards can now be used to pay for essentials such as groceries and rent.

- Credit card companies offer low initial interest rates to entice borrowers to transfer balances from other cards. However, the rates then increase considerably, usually after only six months.

- Many companies, like GE Capital Services, are now charging penalty fees to customers who do not carry a balance on their credit card.

- Credit card companies normally require minimum payments of only 3% of the outstanding balance. But that means the typical $3,900 balance, at 18% interest, would take nearly 42 years to pay off, and those monthly payments would total $14,530.44.

- Capital One advertises they'll lower your minimum payment from 3% to 2% for a fee. What they don't tell you is that paying only 2% of your outstanding balance each month could make the bill last longer than you do.

- People commonly borrow against their home equity. United Jersey Bank advertises that you can make minimum payments, only on interest, for up to ten years. Imagine, ten years could pass, you could pay thousands of dollars, and still have made NO progress on reducing your loan.

- Banc One is planning to test Visa and MasterCard accounts that will allow you to borrow up to 40% of your 401(k) plan before retirement. Nothing like throwing away your future for a little immediate gratification.

Did You Know?

Every dollar you pay above the minimum monthly payment on a debt earns you a gain equivalent to the interest rate the debt charges. In other words, if you pay an extra $100 toward the balance of a credit card that charges 15% interest, you're getting the wealth building effect of earning 15% annually on that $100. That's way better than most investments average over time. So the more you prepay against debt balances (without adding to them at the same time) the more you earn in effective interest.

Prepaying your mortgage balance earns you more than you could possibly lose, in terms of the mortgage interest tax deduction. Let's say you're in the 28% tax bracket. That means the government gives you a 28-cent tax break for every dollar you spend on mortgage interest. But that means you're LOSING 72 cents out of each of those dollars. If anyone tells you that paying a dollar to get back 28 cents is a good investment, suggest they recheck their math.

Appendix B: Suggested Reading

The Millionaire Next Door by Thomas J. Stanley and William D. Danko

The Word on Finances by Larry Burkett

The Seven Habits of Highly Effective People by Stephen R. Covey

Multiple Streams of Income by Robert G. Allen

Faith Raising vs. Money Raising by George O. McCalep, Jr., Ph.D.

www.hesaiditididit.com

www.myfico.com

www.dallasfed.org

www.bankrate.com

www.personalfinancemastery.com